Early Praise for

KNOWING MY FATHER

"Joe Tedeschi has produced a great piece of work describing and highlighting the terrible events of March 24, 1918, when so many merchant seamen risked and lost their lives in a disastrous collision at sea during the Great War. In paying testament to his father, Joe has vividly exposed the price paid by these men, amid the survival of his own father in the catastrophe."

—Dave Wendes, owner of Wight Spirit Diving Charters and author of *South Coast Shipwrecks Off East Dorset & Wight 1870–1979*

"Joseph Tedeschi's book, *Knowing My Father: The Collision of the O. B. Jennings and War Knight*, is an excellent example of how meticulous research can illuminate how humans react when placed in wartime situations. The inclusion of the first-hand transcripts of some of the survivors paints a haunting picture of the harrowing conditions they faced at sea as both ships became engulfed in flames following the collision. Although there is no direct testimony from his father, Joe Tedeschi could easily imagine what his father experienced, and how that shaped his life as he eventually transitioned from wartime to civilian life. Although Joe lost his father at an early age while still in high school, his deep feelings for him shine through at the end of the book. 'Well done, Poppa, well done.'"

—Jack Bartley, former Navy officer and Vietnam veteran, author of *Public Ed – A Novel*, *Smoke on the Water*, **and** *Hilo Dome*

"In *Knowing My Father*, Joe Tedeschi gives us a multifaceted gift. First, he takes us on a poignant journey to meet and salute his long-deceased father. He also provides a painstakingly researched account of a naval tragedy set against the wider scope of a world war. He relates a compelling military story of sacrifice, courage, and heroism. He tells a touching family story of patriotism and resilience that helps us understand our country and the people who help to build it. For those who have read Joe's previous book, *A Rock in the Clouds*, he gives another opportunity to admire an accomplished author's intellectual curiosity, wisdom, and extraordinary humanity. Lastly, he invites us, as we write the final chapters of our own life stories, to reflect on the legacy we are leaving to others, both loved ones and strangers."

—Bill McCusker, founder and CEO of Fathers & Families, Inc.

"I found great interest in the recounting of the author's detailed, painstaking research of news, records, and documents regarding his father's personal and military life. This work is a labor of love that will capture the reader's undivided attention from beginning to end!"

—Brig. Gen. Ray Ong, Philippine Army, West Point class of 1963

"One son's journey to which all sons and daughters can relate. Well-documented and well-illustrated. Bravo, Zulu Col. Tedeschi!"

—Capt. GS Wysocki, JAGC USNR (Ret.)

Knowing My Father
The Collision of the O. B. Jennings *and* War Knight

by Col. Joseph R. Tedeschi, US Army (Ret.)

© Copyright 2025 Col. Joseph R. Tedeschi, US Army (Ret.)

ISBN 979-8-88824-819-5

All rights reserved. No part of this publication may be reproduced, stored in a retrieval system, or transmitted in any form or by any means—electronic, mechanical, photocopy, recording, or any other—except for brief quotations in printed reviews, without the prior written permission of the author.

Published by
◤köehlerbooks™

3705 Shore Drive
Virginia Beach, VA 23455
800-435-4811
www.koehlerbooks.com

KNOWING MY FATHER

THE COLLISION OF THE
O. B. JENNINGS AND *WAR KNIGHT*

COL. JOSEPH R. TEDESCHI
US ARMY (RET.)

VIRGINIA BEACH
CAPE CHARLES

To my father; my mother, Rose;
my sister, Theresa; and my brother, Mike.

They that go down to the sea in ships,
that do business in great waters;
These see the works of the L ORD,
and his wonders in the deep.
Psalm 107:23–24 KJV

CONTENTS

Prologue 1

PART ONE: Gaining Insights into My Father 5
   Chapter 1: Developing the Story 7
   Chapter 2: Military Service Records 14

PART TWO: The Year 1917, Going to War 19
   Chapter 3: Joining Up and Initial Training 21
   Chapter 4: Merchant Ships Serve in the War 26

PART THREE: The Year 1918, Peril at Sea 33
   Chapter 5: The Crisis of Allied Merchant Shipping 35
   Chapter 6: Convoy HN53 39
   Chapter 7: Set Up for Disaster 43
   Chapter 8: A Catastrophe in the Making 46
   Chapter 9: Firsthand Testimonies of the Collision on
      O. B. Jennings 51
   Chapter 10: The Collision As Experienced
      on the *War Knight* 55
   Chapter 11: The Immediate Aftermath of the Collision ... 77
   Chapter 12: Accountability for the Collision 79
   Chapter 13: Final Disposition of the Ships 93
   Chapter 14: My Father's Succeeding Naval Assignments ... 98
   Chapter 15: After the War 108
   Chapter 16: Knowing My Father 112

Acknowledgments 115

PROLOGUE

I never really knew my father, Michael Angelo Tedeschi. He died in 1951 when I was seventeen years old and just starting my last year of high school. Having lost him when I was a teenager, I have so little of his true self to hang on to. As I grew older and experienced more of life and fatherhood myself, I began to recognize and feel this missing part of my life. Over the years, I also developed an intense desire to learn more about my father, to know him better even in retrospect.

At the outset, I don't want my feelings toward my father misunderstood. I loved him dearly. He was a good family man, loyal and faithful to his wife and children. He provided for his family (we owned our home and an automobile), and during my early childhood at the height of the Depression years, he worked hard as a truck driver for a beer distributorship. At the beginning of World War II, he took a civil-service job maintaining aircraft armament with the US Navy at Quonset Point Naval Air Station in Rhode Island. By the standards of that time, our family would have been considered lower middle class. We had all the necessities, but we never took a family vacation.

My father had a strong bond and relationship with his oldest child, my sister Theresa, and was immensely proud to see her graduate from college. He worked diligently with my mother to take my brother, Mike Jr., through a difficult childhood and adolescence complicated by a birth injury to his right arm. As the youngest child, I tagged along with all the tensions, dynamics, and interactions of family life and slipped through adolescence with almost no paternal guidance, direction, or mentorship.

I certainly could have used some during that confusing time of my life. The years directly preceding and following my father's death were particularly difficult for me. When I needed and wanted my father most, his death robbed me of him. As I look back on it now, despite a normal and healthy relationship with my father, there simply was neither sufficient time nor opportunity to really get to *know* him.

I don't remember ever bantering or sharing a joke with my father. I've lamented and felt cheated by this all my life, especially as I experienced fatherhood myself and established relationships with my own two daughters. I was particularly pained by his absence during my last year of high school when I captained the football team through a championship season, and even more so upon graduation when I pondered an uncertain future.

For many reasons, I needed to fill this gap in my life, and it occurred to me that if I knew more about my father's early life before he married my mother in 1925, I might be able to get to know him better and fill in parts of this absence. My intentions were to write a memoir of sorts about his life, one that might be fulfilling for me and possibly illuminate a dark chapter of my life.

I began my research for this project by exploring his early life through various ancestry search engines. I was very successful in gathering a comprehensive account of his early life from these records until the year 1917 when he enlisted in the US Navy. From that point on, I researched his World War I military service records for more information on his life and background. In doing so, I discovered the remarkable and tragic story of the 1918 collision of the *O. B. Jennings*, a US merchant ship on which my father was a Navy armed guard, with the British merchant ship *War Knight*. This discovery piqued my curiosity, and I researched the story extensively. My findings opened up a whole new world of related interest in Allied merchant shipping during World War I and how and why the US Navy began to place armed guards on their merchant ships.

My research unearthed intriguing new information about my father, revealing parts of his life and character I never knew. In doing so, I also discovered a story only minimally covered by the media—the day two Allied merchant ships tragically collided during World War I. My new discovery inspired me to add the story of this collision to the memoir about my father.

PART ONE

Gaining Insights into My Father

PART ONE

CHAPTER 1

Developing the Story

My investigation into my father's most perilous experience in World War I revealed three protagonists: Michael Angelo Tedeschi, gunner's mate second class, member of the US Navy Armed Guard; the US merchant ship *O. B. Jennings*; and the British merchant ship *War Knight*. To weave the story between my father and the two ships, I became a willing fourth protagonist, albeit a passive one, as part of my desire and search to know my father better.

My purpose in combining these stories into a book is to relate how these three protagonists came together at approximately 2:30 a.m. on Sunday, March 24, 1918, when the *O. B. Jennings* and *War Knight*, traveling in convoy HN53B, collided at sea.

Both ships were set ablaze and critically damaged. The *War Knight* had a crew of forty-seven men, and only eleven survived the collision (three died later from injuries). The seventy-two members of the *O. B. Jennings* crew abandoned ship and were heroically rescued at sea with the loss of only one man. My father was one of those rescued, as the sea burned from the cargo of naphtha fuel carried by the *O. B. Jennings*.

Numerous ships and men were lost at sea during World War I, and this is but one of many stories of such tragedies. However, this story is particularly important to me—if my father had *not* survived the collision, I would not be here 105 years later to retell the story!

MY FATHER'S EARLY LIFE FROM 1894 TO 1917

Since my father is the living link between the two inanimate ship protagonists, and as part of my search to know my father better, I will begin this story by relating as much as I could discover about my father's life until 1917.

To meaningfully know my father's life, I needed to revisit or at least imagine the world in which he was born and lived up to the time he joined the Navy at twenty-two years of age in 1917. I was able to somewhat recreate his early years from ancestry search engines and census records, which provided important information about his parents and family.

His father, Giuseppe (Joseph) Tedeschi, immigrated to the US from Fornelli, Italy, in May of 1890.

The lure of employment in the expanding cotton textile industry of New England drew many people from Southern Italy to work in the cotton mills, and my grandfather was one of them. The ship *Birmania*'s passenger manifest reveals Giuseppe traveled alone from Italy, which means he left my grandmother, Teresa, and two small children, Ida and Guido, behind in Fornelli (not uncommon—my maternal grandparents did the same thing).

Fig. 1. Fornelli, Italy orientation

Exhaustive searches did not reveal exactly when or how his small family joined Giuseppe in the US, but the US national census of 1900 discloses that they followed him shortly thereafter, sometime in either 1890 or 1891. Records show the family resided in Warwick, Rhode Island, but I have little other specific information about the events in their lives between 1890 and 1900. I had to rely upon the cryptic entries of the census for clues and the information I needed to piece together the very significant events that did take place during those previous ten years.

By 1900, the census records show the Tedeschi family had

increased by four more children after they arrived in the US. Antonio was born in October 1892, and my father, Michael, was born on July 12, 1894, in Westcott, a small subsection of Warwick. A daughter, Maria, was born in February 1896, and a son, Luigi, in July 1899. He was ten months old at the time of the census but died shortly thereafter. The 1900 census also denotes my father Michael "at school" at age six.

By the time of the 1910 US census, my father was sixteen, had completed his schooling up to the fourth grade, and had begun working (at age eight or nine) as a "spinner in cotton mill" at B.B. & R. Knight's Natick mill.[1] The Tedeschi family had grown again during those ten years, with Gina born in 1901, Enrico born in 1904, and the last child, Anna, born in 1905. The oldest daughter, Ida, had married and left the household by 1910, but the census reveals my grandfather and the next four oldest children were all working at the Natick cotton mill to sustain the family. This was an accepted way of life during those years. All the children, despite their ages, were expected to work and support the family household.

CHILD LABOR

Fig. 2. Some of the boys working at Natick mills, RI, Saturday, noon, April 17, 1909

---

[1] Larry Manire, "Natick Mill (destroyed)," Rhode Tour, https://rhodetour.org/items/show/398.

The precisely dated photo of boys outside Natick mill was taken by noted photographer Lewis Wickes Hine as part of the National Child Labor Committee Collection. His photos were critical in supporting the national effort to curb child labor.

Mr. Hine was rarely welcome inside mills or other facilities when he attempted to take photos of the exploited children providing cheap labor. On the occasion of his taking photos at the Natick mill in April 1909, Mr. Hine had to set up his camera tripod and wait outside the mill entrance to entice groups of child workers to pose for photographs.

In the photo, Mr. Hine was able to group these boys as they exited the mill for their lunch break. Innocent and guileless as to why the photo was being taken, the boys were probably curious and even flattered that someone would want to take their picture. While the boys are not identified, I feel quite certain that the boy second from left is my father. His facial features match exactly, and by April 1909, he would have been fourteen years old. I was able to partially confirm his likeness with 63 percent confidence using the facial-comparison AI tool FaceShape.

By the time of the 1915 Rhode Island census, at twenty-one years old, my father was still listed as working as "spinner in cotton mill," which means he had been at that same job for fourteen or fifteen years. Two years later, on April 5, 1917, the US declared war on Germany, and my father "joined up" a week later, April 12, 1917, to serve his country in the Navy. He was twenty-two going on twenty-three.

MOTIVATION FOR "JOINING UP"

I'm compelled to ponder what my father's motivations were for voluntarily enlisting in the US Navy. Patriotism? A chance to break out from the cotton mill and see the world? A case of better not to wait and eventually be drafted? I can only surmise the reasons, because there are no surviving family members who can enlighten me. My best guess is that he joined up for a combination of reasons.

From what I know of my father, patriotism was certainly a factor. He was the third son of my grandparents, and by this time, I feel a sense of patriotism and loyalty had developed within the Tedeschi family for their new homeland, the United States—despite the prejudice being fostered against Italian immigrants at that time. For example, eleven Italian immigrants had been slaughtered in New Orleans in 1891 by a mob for their alleged role in the murder of the police chief, even after some of them had been acquitted at trial. It was the largest mass lynching in American history. Most of the lynching victims accused in the murder had been rounded up and charged just because of their Italian ethnicity. [2]

Since that tragic event, the tide of prejudice against Italian immigrants has been countermanded and abated by several positive moves. For example, Columbus Day was established as a national holiday in honor of the Italian explorer, although many Italian Americans observe Columbus Day as a celebration of their heritage and not of Columbus himself. By 1917, I'm certain my father had fully accepted his role as a native-born American citizen and was prepared to defend his nation in time of war.

Another factor bearing on his decision to enlist was the understanding within the family that his wages at the cotton mill were important to sustaining a large household consisting of his parents, two older brothers, and three younger siblings. I suspect there might have been some tension in the family about my father enlisting and depriving the family of a source of

---

[2] Erin Blakemore, "The Grisly Story of One of America's Largest Lynching[s]," History.com, October 25, 2017, updated April 15, 2025, https://www.history.com/articles/the-grisly-story-of-americas-largest-lynching.

household income. However, with my father's service allotment to maintain the support of the household, this issue must have been satisfactorily resolved.

Just after my father enlisted, the government called for draft registration, and despite an extensive search, I was not able to find his registration card. I can surmise that his registration was not required because he had already enlisted.

In searching for my father's draft registration card, I discovered records of his two older brothers' registration. Guido and Antonio both registered on the same date and at the same place (the handwritten registration cards were in identical handwriting, surely by the same registration official), but in a confusing revelation, I noticed that both listed a false home address. My presumption is that they did this in an ill-conceived and hasty attempt to avoid the draft, likely not for a lack of patriotism but because they recognized the need to continue supporting the striving household.

As it turned out, my Uncle Guido (Jimmy) was later drafted and served honorably in the Army's 303rd Engineers, experiencing a year of frontline–combat engineer action in France. My Uncle Antonio (Tony) was eventually excused from the draft because of a congenital arm infirmity.

Walking in his shoes, I feel certain my father was motivated by patriotism, a sense of adventure, and a chance to break out from the cotton mill and see the world. I know that's what I would have done.

CHAPTER 2

— ★ —

Military Service Records

My first source for my father's military service rested on an honored shelf in my home. An unofficial record of his service was made part of the frontispiece of a set of books on World War I published by the American Legion after the war. These volumes had been proudly displayed on our family bookcase for many years.

Fig. 3. Copy of my father's unofficial service record prepared by the American Legion

I'm not certain where the information for this record was gathered and compiled by the American Legion, possibly with some input from my father when he ordered the book set. It reads as follows:

> Entered US Navy April 12, 1917, at Newport, RI, as Seaman. Assigned to US Battleship *New Hampshire*. Transferred to oil tanker *O. B. Jennings*, Standard Oil Ship, as a member of the Gunners Crew, which on 24 March 1918, on fourth trip was torpedoed by a German submarine and rammed by His Majesty's ship *Man of War* off the Isle of Wight in the English Channel. Was one of the crew picked up by the British Destroyer *Garland*. Was taken to the Victory Station at Portsmouth, England, and later transferred to the Bay Ridge Brooklyn Navy Yard and assigned to the *Lake Harney* at Montreal. Sailed to Rochefort, France, where ship was assigned to transportation service between Ireland, Wales, England, and France. After serving for some time on this ship, was transferred to the USS *Philippine* transporting troops back to the US until date of discharge. Discharged from service Oct 20, 1919, at Newport, RI, as Gunners Mate, Second Class.

My later research would disclose that some parts of the information in this record are in complete error. I was able to compare this record with the official Navy War Service Certificate of his service, which he obtained when he was discharged. The certificate was passed to me by my mother after my father's death. The record is difficult to read because my father folded and kept it in his wallet for many years after the war.

Fig. 4. Official War Service Certificate of my father's service in the US Navy

The certificate, recording only the commissioned US Navy ships and stations where he served, reads as follows:

No. 199909

War Service Certificate
United States Navy
103-69-67

This is to certify that Michael Angelo Tedeschi GM2/c, U.S.N. performed honorable active service in the United States Navy from 12 April 1917 to 18 October 1919 on board the following ships and stations:

Naval Training Camp, Portsmouth, New Hampshire;

USS *New Hampshire*: R.S. at Norfolk: Armed Draft Detail, New York, NY; USS *Lake Harney*: Naval Base, Cardiff: R.S. at New York; USS *Philippine*: Naval Training Station, Newport, Rhode Island.

"R.S." is a navy abbreviation for "receiving ship," which means temporarily holding and administering personnel between assignments. My father's time on the *O. B. Jennings* is recorded under "R.S. at Norfolk: Armed Draft Detail, New York, N.Y." The *O. B. Jennings* is not named in this certificate because it was a merchant ship and not a commissioned US Navy ship.

My father's naval service records gave me intriguing but cryptic insights into his early life and piqued my curiosity. What was hidden among the static, official language of these records? In particular, I was fascinated and curious to know much more about the part of his unofficial military service record that read:

> Transferred to oil tanker *O. B. Jennings*, Standard Oil Ship as a member of the Gunner's Crew, which on 24 March 1918, on fourth trip was torpedoed by a German submarine and rammed by His Majesty's ship *Man of War* off the Isle of Wight in the English Channel. Was one of the crew picked up by the British Destroyer *Garland*. Was taken to the Victory Station at Portsmouth, England.

All I ever knew of this part of my father's life had been gathered from family lore. In broad strokes, my father had been in the Navy during World War I and his ship had been sunk in the English Channel. I remember being told that he was rescued from the water set ablaze by burning gasoline and that he was picked from the water by a British ship. He had lost everything he possessed on the sunken ship, and the

British took care of him—even outfitting him temporarily with a British Navy uniform.

Pictures of my father wearing the British Navy uniform and another faded one of him wearing the US Navy uniform are the only photographic record I have of his World War I service. That's all I ever knew and understood about my father's wartime naval action, and I grew up and lived with this story all my life, the details buried in history.

UNLOCKING THE PAGES OF HISTORY

In my ninetieth year of life, I decided to investigate and research the real story of my father's time on the *O. B. Jennings*, its sinking in the English Channel, and his rescue at sea. I hoped to pry more of this story from the buried pages of history and learn more about my father at the same time. With the help of internet search engines and, most recently, with the aid of the artificial intelligence Google search engine, Bard (now Gemini), I was able to piece together an accurate and comprehensive account of what really happened to my father while aboard the tanker *O. B. Jennings*.

The true story differs in significant details from what is written in his brief service records. I discovered fascinating military history during my research—stories and records of brave men manning ships at war, the fledgling convoy system, the scourge of submarine warfare, the risks of transporting liquid fuel in ships, and the camaraderie of allies during WWI, particularly the US and Britain. My findings were extensive and intriguing. They had all the makings of a book that not only completed parts of my father's life for me but also revealed one of many tragic events that did take place during the war.

PART TWO

The Year 1917

Going to War

Fig. 5. The Boston Globe, April 17, 1917

CHAPTER 3

★

Joining Up and Initial Training

My father's enlistment came at a time very early in the US involvement in World War I when patriotic fervor was running very high, a wave of enthusiasm recorded in the upbeat tone of newspapers of the day. For example, the newspaper account in *The Boston Globe* on April 17, 1917, captures the mood at the Navy recruiting center on 146 Tremont Street in Boston, where my father was formally inducted into the Navy.

The lead to the article sets the tone: "Secure 59 New Bluejackets / Speeding Up the Naval Enlistments / Lightweight Champion of Navy Big Aid in Recruiting." Having the US Navy's lightweight boxing champion on the scene was clearly a plus to aid more recruitment. A list of each enlistee's name, neighborhood, and city follows the final heading, "Yankee Peacemakers Enlisting April 16." My father's name is among the list of fifty-nine new recruits: "Michael A. Tedeschi, Prospect Hill, Natick, RI."

I am not certain exactly where my father was sent to Navy boot camp. His unofficial American Legion record indicates he was sent to Newport, Rhode Island, for training. His official Navy War Certificate of Service states he was sent to Naval Training Camp, Portsmouth, New Hampshire. He went through ten to twelve weeks of required basic training followed by selection for his first assignment—the US Navy Armed Guard for merchant ships.

The pressing need to protect merchant shipping from German submarine attacks led to the creation of the Navy Armed Guard. The new and challenging mission drove an urgent need to provide the required manpower and resources to fill this role. The wartime scramble to make this happen caught up with my father just at the time of his enlistment. However, the decision to arm merchant ships was controversial and did not come about easily.

THE CREATION OF THE US NAVY ARMED GUARD

Controversy over the arming of merchant ships was a significant factor in the lead-up to the United States' entry into World War I. It showed that there was a deep divide in American opinion about the war, and it helped to push the country closer to war.

In February 1917, two months before the US entry into the war, President Woodrow Wilson requested authority from Congress to arm American merchant ships with US naval personnel and equipment. The measure, supported by many members of Congress, was opposed by a small group of antiwar senators who filibustered the bill, preventing it from coming to a vote.[3]

In the end, President Wilson decided to arm merchant ships by executive order, claiming that an old anti-piracy law gave him the authority to do so. This decision was controversial, but the Supreme Court ultimately upheld it.[4] The country formally established the US Navy Armed Guard in 1917, shortly after the United States entered World War I and my father's enlistment in the Navy. Their mission was to defend merchant ships from attack by German submarines and surface raiders.

---

[3] "U.S. Entry into World War I, 1917," Milestones: 1914–1920, US Department of State Office of the Historian, https://history.state.gov/milestones/1914-1920/wwi.

[4] US Department of State Office of the Historian, "U.S. Entry into World War I, 1917."

The selection and training of armed guards in World War I was not as rigorous as it would be in World War II. The Navy was in a hurry to get men trained and on merchant ships. The basic training for armed guards lasted for about six weeks. It included instruction in gunnery, seamanship, and military discipline. After basic training, armed guards were assigned to merchant ships and made responsible for manning the ship's guns and for taking other measures to defend their assigned ship from attack.

TRAINING ON THE BATTLESHIP *NEW HAMPSHIRE*
The Navy's urgent need to train men in the duties of the newly formed armed guards had to begin right away, despite the lack of any existing facilities or training centers. Until more permanent arrangements could be established, the Navy used the battleship *New Hampshire* as a temporary training platform for the armed guards. It served for the next eighteen months following the declaration of war to train gunners for the rapidly expanding wartime fleet.

My father's service record indicates he was assigned to the battleship *New Hampshire* following boot camp. Since the record does not list dates, I can assume it occurred around July 1917 after his ten to twelve weeks of boot camp. I am also assuming he stayed with the *New Hampshire* just long enough—possibly six weeks—to be trained as an armed guard. During that short period of time, he had a picture of himself taken with the *New Hampshire* cap band just barely visible in the faded photo. (All cap ribbons bearing the ship name were later replaced with "US Navy" during the war for security reasons.)[5]

---

[5] Recorder, Permanent Naval Uniform Board, to Secretary, Permanent Naval Uniform Board, April 10, 1953, reprinted in United States, Bureau of Naval Personnel, BUPERSNOTE 1020, December 19, 1983, https://www.history.navy.mil/research/library/online-reading-room/title-list-alphabetically/u/uniforms-usnavy/hats-caps.html.

Fig. 6. Photo of my father with the USS New Hampshire cap band

ASSIGNMENT TO THE *O. B. JENNINGS*

Following his training as an armed guard on the *New Hampshire*, my father was assigned to the oil tanker *O. B. Jennings* as part of the US Navy Armed Guard draft detail. The details and timing of this transfer are not certain, but I can ascertain it took place after his armed guard training and his temporary assignment to "Receiving Ship at Norfolk."[6]

The *New Hampshire*'s home base was in Norfolk, Virginia, and it's reasonable to assume my father was held at the receiving ship at Norfolk for a short period in anticipation of the launching of the *O. B. Jennings* on October 31, 1917, from nearby Newport News. I suspect the formal transfer to the *O. B. Jennings* took place in the November time frame.

The American Legion service record states my father made four trips on the *O. B. Jennings* transferring oil overseas before the collision with the *War Knight* took place. This seems plausible, since a round trip took about a month. This could then allow time for four trips between November 1917 and March 1918.

---

[6] See official War Service Certificate on page 16.

CHAPTER 4

★

Merchant Ships Serve in the War

The *O. B. Jennings* and the *War Knight* are such significant parts of this narrative, it's important to understand what kind of ships they were and the role they played in my father's survival when they collided in March of 1918. Both were newly launched ships in 1917, and both served less than a year before being lost to the sea in 1918.

THE LAUNCH OF THE *O. B. JENNINGS*

Anticipating the need for oil tankers to transport critically needed fuel for the war effort, the Standard Oil Company of New Jersey had ordered seven ships to be built between 1916 and 1917 by Newport News Shipbuilding and Drydock Company, Newport News, Virginia. The *O. B. Jennings*, the last of these ships to be built, was launched on October 31, 1917. The ship was named after Oliver Burr Jennings, one of the original founders of the Standard Oil Company.

The brand-new ship was immediately put in service and likely made its maiden voyage overseas in November 1917, the first of the four voyages on record. I assume, too, that the ship's merchant crew was augmented on each voyage with a detail from the newly formed US Navy Armed Guard, which included my father on his initial Armed Guard assignment.

Fig. 7. SS O. B. Jennings (American merchant tanker)

The *O. B. Jennings* in this photo is painted in dazzle camouflage designed to break up the hull outlines, making it difficult for a submarine to get an accurate fix on the vessel and determine its size, outline, speed, and course. The dazzle camouflage may also have been an unfortunate factor in delayed recognition between ships before the fatal collision of the *O. B. Jennings* and *War Knight*.

The *O. B. Jennings* was a steam-propelled oil tanker registering 10,290 gross tons. The ship had a length of four hundred feet and a beam—the width of a ship at its widest point—of fifty feet. Its steel double hull was engineered to make it more resistant to damage from enemy attacks or explosions. It stored oil in a series of steel tanks below deck designed to withstand the pressure of the oil and to prevent leaks. At the time of its launch, the *O. B. Jennings* was the world's largest oil tanker, essentially a floating gasoline transport container in the shape of a ship.

Being a merchant tanker, the *O. B. Jennings* was commanded by a master (George W. Nordston on the fourth voyage when the collision occurred) and a merchant marine crew of fifty men. The Naval Armed Guard on the voyage of the collision consisted of a chief warrant officer who commanded twenty-two Navy ratings manning guns (including my father) and three Navy wireless operators.

MAKING A NEW CONCEPT HAPPEN

With any large-scale, complex, and novel innovation like placing Navy armed guards on merchant vessels, there has to be considerable planning, coordination, and certainly some friction to make it happen. While the US government, the US Navy, and the merchant marine world all saw the dire need to do this, there still had to be formal legal procedures and arrangements put in place to move forward. Considering the wartime exigencies, these efforts proved a remarkable accomplishment and a tribute to all that made it work.

I have no specific information about the first time my father's contingent of the US Navy Armed Guard interfaced with the master and crew of the *O. B. Jennings*, but I have to assume that it took place after lengthy effort and coordination to customize the amount and types of armament for the *O. B. Jennings*. The two parties had to negotiate logistics and quartering of the Navy contingent, establish command lines between the master of the merchant ship and the commander of the Navy Armed Guard, and resolve a myriad of other interface issues.

I can imagine it took time to smooth the issues that surfaced, especially on the maiden voyage. We can assume by the time of the fourth voyage, many of these issues were ironed out and that a good relationship was in place between the master and crew of the *O. B. Jennings* and its armed guard. The testimony of George W. Nordston, master of the *O. B. Jennings*, recorded in the UK Admiralty Court of Enquiry investigating the collision of the *O. B. Jennings* and the *War Knight* indicates that they had achieved a good relationship as such.[7]

By the end of 1917, the *O. B. Jennings* had completed one or two voyages transporting oil from the US to England. I want to believe my father was becoming a seasoned sailor by this time and had satisfactorily integrated himself as a member of the US Navy Armed Guard on the *O. B. Jennings*.

THE LAUNCH OF THE *WAR KNIGHT*

Having been at war since 1914, the British government had already lost a considerable number of merchant ships by 1917 and had a critical need to replace them as soon as possible. To accomplish this, they established the standard-built ships program.[8] The aim of the program was to standardize ships into a simple design with similar hulls and engines (much like the US did with the Liberty Ship program in World War II). Each ship in the program would be named starting with the prefix "War," and they came to be known as the "war-prefix" class of ships. Naming ships in this manner led to some amusing and interesting juxtapositions such as *War Crocus* and *War Tune*. By the end of the war, around 600–650 ships of various classes would be built, all with the prefix "War" in their names.

---

[7] You may find images of his testimony at my website, joetedeschi.com/uk-natl-archives-court-of-enquiry/. *Court of Enquiry Order 0197/62 into Supposed Loss of US* O. B. Jennings *and* War Knight, April 3–6, 1918, 506–515.

[8] Ted Finch and Gilbert Provost, "WWI Standard Built Ships," Mariners, http://www.mariners-l.co.uk/WWlStandardBuilt.htm.

In the initial stages of the program, ships were purchased that were already being constructed, so early examples of the war-prefix vessels did not all fit the simple design of later ships. This included the *War Knight*.

Fig. 8. War Knight *at the launch (Harry Courtright, Commercial Photo View—Union Iron Works, 1917. Gelatin silver print, glass, linen. Collection of the Oakland Museum of California. Gift of Herrington & Olson.)*

The *War Knight* was built by Union Iron Works in California and launched in December 1917.[9] It was designed as a steam-propelled transport ship for cargo with eight thousand gross

---

[9] *Forgotten Wrecks of the First World War, SS* War Knight *Site Report* (Maritime Archeology Trust, 2018), 7, https://maritimearchaeologytrust.org/wp-content/uploads/2021/01/FWFWW_WarKnight_SiteReport.pdf.

register tonnage. The ship had a length of 410 feet and a beam of 56 feet. The London-based firm Furness, Withy & Co. owned the ship, and it was operated at the time of the collision by the shipping controller, one of the new positions created by the British government in 1916 to regulate and organize merchant shipping to supply the United Kingdom with the materials needed to fight the war.[10]

Being a merchant ship like the *O. B. Jennings*, the *War Knight* was commanded by a master (Captain Holroyd during the voyage when the collision occurred) and a merchant marine crew of forty-seven men. While the British Navy employed an armed guard aboard some of their merchant ships during World War I, the program was not as extensive as the US Navy Armed Guard program. By the end of the war, the British had over two thousand armed merchant ships in service. The guns were manned by Royal Navy crews who were trained to fire at submarines and surface raiders. However, at the time of the collision with the *O. B. Jennings*, the *War Knight* did not have any Royal Navy armed guards on board.

I could find no service record of the *War Knight* after it was launched at the end of 1917. I can assume it was put to sea immediately and employed in various aspects of the merchant marine service in support of the British government war effort.

RECAP FOR THE YEAR 1917

By the end of 1917, both the *O. B. Jennings* and *War Knight* had been newly launched and in active service on the high seas. Gunner's Mate Second Class Michael A. Tedeschi, newly enlisted in the US Navy and serving in the US Navy Armed Guard on

---

[10] "The Discovery Service," Records inherited and created by the Ministry of Transport, Shipping Divisions | The National Archives, August 12, 2009, https://discovery.nationalarchives.gov.uk/details/r/C874.

the *O. B. Jennings*, had made one or two voyages delivering oil overseas in support of the Allied war effort.

I would like to believe by this time my father had made any adjustments needed to integrate himself into all the new and stressful wartime environments he was experiencing. It all must have been quite a culture shock for him to go from a spinner in a cotton mill to a US Navy sailor on the high seas under wartime conditions. He certainly was seeing the world, which was part of the adventure I believe he sought.

PART THREE

The Year 1918

Peril at Sea

CHAPTER 5

The Crisis of Allied Merchant Shipping

The Allies began 1918 with determination to win, but eventual victory remained elusive and still very much uncertain. The war was bogged down on the battlefields of Europe, and huge quantities of men and supplies were needed by the Allies to break this stalemate.

Being in the war since 1914, Great Britain had completely mobilized their merchant fleet to support acquisition and delivery of needed manpower and supplies from all over the world. The United States contributed by providing critical manpower and matériel to the war effort and delivering this aid to ports in England and France through a massive recruitment and restructuring of their own merchant fleet. The *O. B. Jennings*, the *War Knight*, and my father were now part of this massive effort to deliver men and supplies to Europe, and they joined the large number of merchant-ship convoys crossing the perilous Atlantic in support of the war effort.

In fact, the merchant-shipping support of the Allied war effort was precarious in January 1918. Unrestricted submarine warfare had been called off twice during the war to avoid drawing the US into the conflict, but it resumed in February

1917.[11] In that year, German submarines sank over six million tons of Allied shipping, and the situation was only getting worse.

The Allies were heavily dependent on merchant shipping to transport troops, supplies, and ammunition to the war zones. If the submarine could continue to sink ships at the same rate, it would be difficult for the Allies to sustain their war effort.

The Allies took a number of steps to try to protect their shipping. They established convoys of merchant ships escorted by warships. They also developed new anti-submarine technologies, such as depth charges[12] and an early-stage sonar system.[13] However, these measures were not always effective, and German submarines continued to sink ships.

Entering the war in April 1917, the United States' participation helped to turn the tide of the shipping crisis. The US Navy provided escorts for Allied convoys, and US shipbuilders began to produce new merchant ships at a rapid pace. However, the shipping crisis of early 1918 was a serious threat to the Allied war effort.

In January 1918, submarines had sunk over one million tons of Allied shipping in December 1917 alone, and the rate of sinkings was continuing to increase. The Allies were struggling to keep up with the demand for shipping, and there were concerns that they would not be able to transport enough troops and supplies to the war zones to win the conflict.

---

[11] David Mishan, "Did the Convoy System Save Britain in World War I?" The Collector, February 12, 2025, https://www.thecollector.com/convoy-system-save-britain-in-world-war-i/.
[12] Mishan, "Did the Convoy System Save Britain in World War I?"
[13] Mark Milligan, "Rutherford's Secret WW1 Mission Helped Pioneer 'Sonar'," *Heritage Daily*, November 9, 2014, https://www.heritagedaily.com/2014/11/rutherfords-secret-ww1-mission-helped-pioneer-sonar/105463.

THE CONVOY SYSTEM

Of the various ways being developed to protect Allied merchant shipping from attack by German submarines and surface raiders, the convoy system was proving to be the most effective.[14] However, the demanding and complex convoy system was still evolving at the beginning of 1918.

The convoy system consisted of groups of merchant ships sailing together under the protection of warships. Convoys typically consisted of ten to fifty merchant ships escorted by a group of warships, which included cruisers, destroyers, and armed trawlers. The warships provided a variety of defensive capabilities, including anti-submarine weapons, guns, and an early form of sonar.[15] The convoys also used a variety of tactics to make it more difficult for submarines to attack them, such as dazzle camouflage,[16] sailing in zigzag patterns, and changing course frequently.

The warship escorts were responsible for protecting the merchant ships from submarine attacks and surface raiders. Convoys were typically organized into three columns, with the warships on the flanks and at the front and rear of the convoy. Convoys sailed at a set speed chosen to be slow enough for all the merchant ships in the convoy to keep up but fast enough to make it difficult for submarines to intercept the convoy.

The convoy system was initially resisted by some Allied naval

---

[14] "British Naval Convoy System Introduced," History.com, October 28, 2009, https://www.histo ry.com/this-day-in-history/may-24/british-naval-convoy-system-introduced; Mishan, "Did the Convoy System Save Great Britain in WWI?"

[15] "The Revolutionary WWI Convoy System That Outsmarted the Deadly German U-Boats," History Skills, https://www.historyskills.com/classroom/year-9/wwi-convoy-system/.

[16] Linda Batchelor, "Dazzling Displays," National Maritime Museum Cornwall, https://nmmc.co.uk/2022/04/dazzling-displays/.

commanders and merchant-ship captains. They were concerned that sailing in a convoy would make them more vulnerable to attack. They also believed the convoys were inflexible and too slow and cumbersome to manage. It was especially difficult to organize and manage large convoys. However, the devastation of the submarine campaign in 1917 forced the Allies to adopt the convoy system on a large scale.

By the beginning of 1918, the convoy system was in full operation. Convoys were sailing from North America to Europe, from South America to Europe, and from Africa to Europe. The convoy system was also being used to protect shipping in the Mediterranean Sea and the North Sea. In January 1918, there were two main convoy routes in the Atlantic Ocean. The first route ran from North America to the United Kingdom. The second route ran from South America to the United Kingdom. British warships typically escorted convoys on the North American route. American warships typically escorted convoys on the South American route.

I encourage readers to view the film *Greyhound* starring Tom Hanks released in 2020 to gain an understanding of the scope and size of convoy operations and the perils convoys faced. While the movie is set in early World War II, the tactics used are essentially the same as those developed during World War I.

CHAPTER 6

─ ★ ─

Convoy HN53

The narrative of our three protagonists comes together on March 8, 1918, when Convoy HN53 was formed and sailed from Halifax, Nova Scotia, Canada. The convoy consisted of thirty-two merchant ships including the *O. B. Jennings* and the *War Knight*, escorted by the British Royal Navy ships *Caradoc*, *Calgarian*, and *Caledon*. The convoy was expected to arrive in Liverpool, England, on March 23, 1918.

My father must have become quite familiar with the process and procedure of preparing a ship for convoy since this was his fourth voyage on the *O. B. Jennings*. He certainly was seeing many new places and seaports all over the world—a far cry from his small cotton-mill village in Natick, Rhode Island.

The *O. B. Jennings* was carrying a full cargo of naphtha, a flammable liquid hydrocarbon mixture, in its oil tanks. The naphtha was likely pumped aboard the ship in New York or New Jersey, and then the ship traveled to Halifax to join the convoy.

The *War Knight* was carrying a cargo of 999 tons of case oil (packaged tins of kerosene) in the double bottom of the ship, along with a general cargo of foodstuffs to include bacon and tins of lard, bales of rubber, spruce lumber, and ash. The ship collected its cargo from Philadelphia and New York, then made its way from New York to Halifax on March 5 to the waiting ships for convoy.

It must have taken a considerable amount of planning and coordination among the Allies to assemble thirty-two merchant ships of different nations and their naval escort in one place. Halifax, Nova Scotia, was one of several ports from which convoys were assembled before they departed for Europe.

Once they were on the high seas, Convoy HN53 was divided into two separate convoys designated HN53A and HN53B. The sixteen ships of Convoy HN53A were destined for Liverpool, while the other half of the ships in Convoy HN53B would continue on for ports on the southeastern coast of the UK.

The two recorded reports of this event differ. One report states that the split took place on March 12 at approximately five hundred miles south of Newfoundland. The other report states the convoy split into two parts on March 13 approximately three hundred miles south of Newfoundland. A possible explanation for the difference between the two accounts was the difficulty in 1918 of determining the exact location of convoys in the open ocean.

Both convoys proceeded to an area of the Atlantic Ocean off the coast of England and Ireland known as the Western Approaches. It was one of the most dangerous shipping lanes in the world during World War I, as it was heavily patrolled by German submarines. When merchant convoys from North America arrived in the Western Approaches, they were met by new escorts from the Royal Navy.

The *O. B. Jennings* and *War Knight* were now part of Convoy HN53B heading for ports on the southeastern coast of the UK. As they approached the Western Approaches, an exchange of escorts took place, and a new set of ships from the Royal Navy took over escort duty. Each time a change of escort took place, the critical issue as to who was in command of the convoy arose.

CONVOY COMMAND AND CONTROL

To gain an understanding of convoy command and control, it's important to know the "rules of the road," the naval customs and procedures that governed such events. Each time a convoy was formed or escorts were changed, it required determination of seniority of rank among the merchant shipmasters and the Royal Navy escort ships.

I learned that the senior merchant marine officer in charge of the merchant ships in the convoy is designated as the commodore, responsible for the overall operation of the convoy, including its course, speed, and defensive maneuvers. The commodore works closely with the senior escort officer (SEO) in command of the warships protecting the convoy. [17]

The commodore's position in the chain of command relative to the SEO is a complex one. The commodore is ultimately responsible for the safety of the merchant ships in the convoy, while the SEO is responsible for the safety of the convoy as a whole. This can lead to some tension between the two officers, as they may have different priorities.

Generally, the commodore has the final say on convoy operations, but he is expected to consult with the SEO on all major decisions. The commodore may also delegate some of his responsibilities to the SEO, such as coordinating the convoy's defensive maneuvers.

In practice, the commodore and SEO work closely together to make decisions that are in the best interests of the convoy as a whole. This requires a high level of cooperation and trust between the two officers.

---

[17] Rear Admiral H. D. Cooke, US Navy (Ret.), "The Atlantic Convoys," *Proceedings* Vol. 76/8/570, August 1950, US Naval Institute, https://www.usni.org/magazines/proceedings/1950/august/atlantic-convoys.

Interviews during the Admiralty Court of Enquiry revealed that this determination never took place for Convoy HN53B, a confused situation which contributed to the collision. The commodore of Convoy HN53B (Captain S. A. Pidgeon) was on the merchant ship *Kia Ora*.[18] The SEO was Commander Maurice B. B. Blackwood, Royal Navy, commanding officer of the destroyer *Syringa*, which was located about a mile in front of the convoy. From all accounts, seniority between the commodore of Convoy HN53B and the SEO was never established. It appears that the commodore delegated by fiat all his responsibilities to SEO Commander Blackwood, who made all the critical decisions concerning course, speed, and defensive maneuvers from the time the Royal Navy began escorting convoy HN53B.

---

[18] Capt. S. A. Pidgeon, "Report on Convoy HN53," UK National Archives, reference ADM137/2553.

CHAPTER 7

Set Up for Disaster

To describe the events leading to the collision of *O. B. Jennings* and *War Knight*, I relied upon contemporary newspaper accounts of the accident and archived reports of both the US Navy and British Navy. My main and most reliable source of information came from the final report of the UK Admiralty Court of Enquiry, which began investigating within days of the collision. I was able to obtain a copy of the original 126-page report dated August 1918 from the UK National Archives.[19]

I draw from all these sources to narrate the course of events for Convoy HN53B from 9:00 p.m. on March 23 to around 2:30 a.m. on March 24, when the *O. B. Jennings* and *War Knight* collided, the ensuing rescue operations, and the final disposition of both ships following the collision.

To start, it's helpful to imagine sixteen merchant ships and seven escort ships attempting to maintain their positions in a grouping two to three nautical miles wide and three to five nautical miles in length at night and without navigation lights. Alterations in course required all the merchant ships to maneuver in a coordinated and synchronized pattern with the bevy of faster naval warships at the front, back, and flanks prodding the merchant ships to stay in formation.

---

[19] You can view the report at my website, JoeTedeschi.com.

To add more challenge, convoys employed zigzag maneuvers designed to protect them from submarines. Three types of zigzag maneuvers were used.

1. Fixed zigzag: This was the most basic form of zigzagging, in which ships would change course by a predetermined angle at regular intervals. The angle of change and the duration of each leg of the zigzag were determined in advance and communicated to all ships in the convoy. This method was relatively easy to implement, but its predictability made it more vulnerable to submariners who could learn the convoy's pattern.

2. Variable zigzag: This was a more complex form of zigzagging, in which the angle of change and the duration of each leg of the zigzag were varied randomly. This made predicting the convoy's course more difficult, but it also required more coordination between ships in the convoy.

3. Sector zigzag: This was a hybrid of the fixed and variable zigzag. In a sector zigzag, ships would change course by a predetermined angle within a predetermined sector. The sector would be changed at regular intervals, but the angle of change would be random. This method was designed to combine the advantages of both fixed and variable zigzagging.

When the visibility is good during the daytime, a fair amount of discipline is maintained and the convoy can remain in formation, but the situation changes dramatically at night, especially under poor visibility and after the running lights of all the ships in the convoy have been extinguished. The ships' dazzle camouflage made recognition at night even more difficult.

Communication among the ships at night becomes critical to maintaining convoy discipline. When communication means are further degraded, for example, restricting the use of wireless and relying only on sight and sound signals, risks rise considerably.

All the above risks were in play on the night of March 23/24, 1918, and under these conditions, the best is called for in the combined knowledge and seamanship of all personnel in the merchant convoy and escort ships. After Convoy HN53B was met by the Royal Navy escort, all accounts point toward a very difficult and confusing set of events and circumstances leading to the collision.

CHAPTER 8

― ★ ―

A Catastrophe in the Making

At 2100 hours on March 23, Convoy HN53B, consisting of sixteen merchant ships in eight columns escorted by HMS *Syringa* and six destroyers, was proceeding on a course of S 86 E. The escort ships were positioned per directions from their commander—Captain D (for "Destroyer"), 4th Flotilla—and located in nearby Plymouth, with the SEO on HMS *Syringa* located about a mile in front of the center column of the convoy.

At 2300, the convoy course was altered to N 75 E, which would take them directly to their rendezvous point at St. Catherine's Lighthouse on the Isle of Wight, approximately forty miles away where a further disassembly of the convoy was planned. All convoy ships were also carrying out sector zigzag, adding to the problems of maintaining positions.

Disposition of merchant ships and RN escorts in Convoy 53B, 23 March 1918

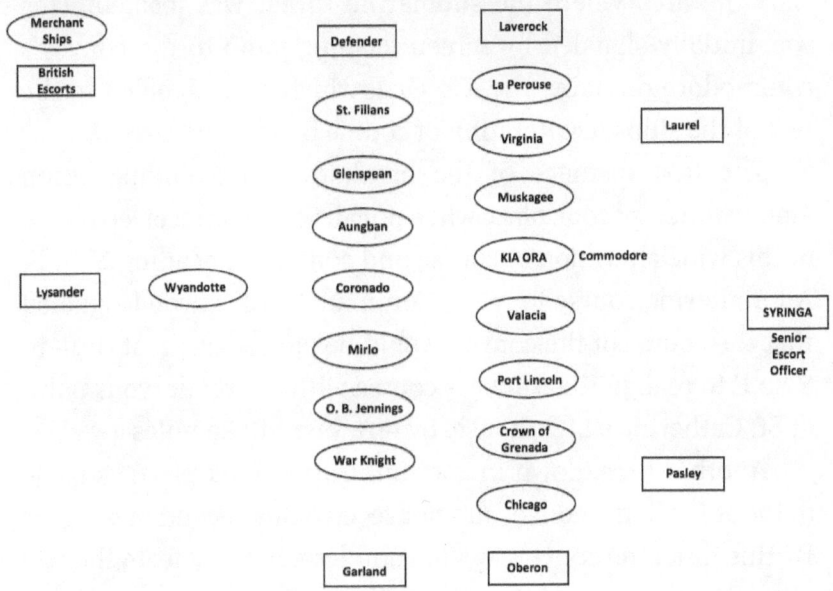

Fig. 9. Disposition of merchant ships and RN escorts in Convoy HN53B, March 23, 1918

Note that the *O. B. Jennings* and *War Knight* were next to each other at this stage of the convoy disposition.

At 0030 on March 24, Commander Blackwood, SEO on the *Syringa*, heard two explosions and saw a flash of light one point (12.5 degrees) on his starboard bow (the right side of the ship as viewed from the bow, the front or forward part of the ship).[20] He judged it was a ship being torpedoed about eight to twelve miles off. [21] If the convoy continued on course, it risked encountering submarines ahead, and after deliberating for thirty minutes (which was later criticized), Commander Blackwood decided to alter course to NNE at about 0100.

---

[20] *Court of Enquiry Order 0197/62 into Supposed Loss of US O. B. Jennings and War Knight*, April 3–6, 1918; UK National Archives, 451.
[21] *Court of Enquiry*, March 25, 1918, 478.

They made this unusually large alteration of course to skirt the area where the submarine threat was located. This was initially signaled by screen flashing lamp to the convoy's commodore directing the *Kia Ora*, which then signaled to the rest of the ships its alteration of course by sound.[22]

The first instance of the breakdown in communication among the ships took place when not all the ships received notice of this wide alteration of course and continued heading N 75 E. After altering course to NNE, Commander Blackwood signaled that the course of the convoy would be altered again at 0215 to S 82 E to realign the convoy's course with the rendezvous point at St. Catherine's Lighthouse, by now just fifteen miles away.[23]

Another breakdown in communication took place as some of the ships in the convoy did not receive this second message.[24] By this time, the convoy was in complete disarray from the two missed messages, and it separated into two groups:

1. A northern portion consisting mainly of the ships which were on the port side (the left side of the ship as viewed from the bow) of the commodore's ship, *Kia Ora*.

2. A southern portion consisting of the remainder of the ships.

The two groups were separated by only a few miles, with the southern group being to the southeast of the northern group. The *Kia Ora* and *War Knight* were now part of the northern group. The *O. B. Jennings*, *Aungban*, and *Mirlo* were part of the southern group.

At this point, Commander Blackwood on *Syringa* recognized that the convoy was in disarray. He sighted the commodore's ship, *Kia Ora*, and attempted to bring the merchant ships back

---

[22] *Court of Enquiry*, March 25, 1918, 479.
[23] *Court of Enquiry*, March 25, 1918, 479.
[24] *Court of Enquiry*, March 25, 1918, 480.

in convoy positions by hailing and closing ships on the *Kia Ora*.

The commander closed on a group of three ships on the original course bearing S 82 E (*O. B. Jennings, Aungban*, and *Mirlo*) and hailed the leading ship, the *O. B. Jennings*. The commander communicated, "Commodore bears about NW, haul up to the Northward."[25] The three ships began the maneuver to close on the *Kia Ora*. Commander Blackwood then hailed the *Valacia*, which was nearby, and told that ship to close on the commodore, but he could not get this ship to obey, causing more delay and confusion.

In the next ten minutes before the collision took place, the *O. B. Jennings*, *Aungban*, and *Mirlo* had closed on the *Kia Ora*, which had the *War Knight* trailing behind her. Both ships appeared to be steering S 82 E. *Aungban* was on the starboard quarter of the *O. B. Jennings* with *Mirlo* on its port beam.

The convoy had been directed to extinguish all running lights, standing operating procedure for navigation in submarine-infested waters,[26] but recognizing the perilous conditions, the *O. B. Jennings*, the *Aungban*, and other ships in the convoy had turned on their navigation lights. In questioning before the Court of Enquiry, George W. Nordston, master of the *O. B. Jennings*,[27] claimed he could see the green navigation lights of the *Kia Ora*. Shortly after, he made out the *War Knight* astern (behind) her and adjusted his bearing to starboard "a point" to pull in behind the commodore's ship and thought he would easily clear the *War Knight*. However, the *War Knight* suddenly turned ninety degrees around on a direct collision course with the *O. B. Jennings*. The *War Knight* struck the *O. B. Jennings* practically at a right angle just behind the bridge on the starboard side.

The bow of the *War Knight* sliced into the double hull of the *O. B. Jennings* and into one of the tanks containing the naphtha

---

[25] *Court of Enquiry*, March 25, 1918, 483.
[26] *Court of Enquiry*, March 25, 1918, 482.
[27] *Court of Enquiry*, March 25, 1918, 506.

cargo. The gas pent up in the tank burst out of the hole in the hull and ignited. This propelled a ball of flame across the deck and bridge of the *War Knight*, instantly killing all who were enveloped by the flames. The release of the pressurized gas was similar to shaking a can of carbonated soft drink before opening, and after releasing the tab, pressurized fizz bursting forth from the opening.

All the elements leading to a wartime catastrophe had come to pass despite all the best planning and thought that went into the safety of convoy HN53B and the convoy system in general. Human limitations and errors, communication breakdown, and the exigencies of the moment overcame the order and discipline needed to prevent this disastrous collision between the *O. B. Jennings* and *War Knight*.

CHAPTER 9

— ★ —

Firsthand Testimonies of the Collision on *O. B. Jennings*

An officer of the *O. B. Jennings* gave the following account of the collision to *The New York Times*:

> "We had an exceptionally rough trip [on crossing the Atlantic]. As a result, the churning of the bulk oil we carried had created a tremendous amount of gas [pressure]. When the *War Knight* hit us there was an instant explosion, caused no doubt by a spark from the impact of the steel setting the gas on fire.
>
> "Immediately, there was a roar of flame spouting out of the hole in the *O. B. Jennings's* side, which all but enveloped the Britisher [*War Knight*]. I learned afterwards that thirty-six of her crew of about fifty were on deck at the time, and they must have been almost instantly incinerated." [28]

Both ships and the surrounding water burst into flames, caused by the burning naphtha pouring from the hole in the side of the *O. B. Jennings*. After the collision, the *O. B. Jennings*

---

[28] "Oil Ship Crash Cost 37 Lives," *New York Times*, August 6, 1918, https://www.nytimes.com/1918/04/18/archives/oil-ship-crash-cost-37-lives-survivors-of-the-ob-jennings-describe.html.

continued in a slow circle to port with the little headway she maintained. The *War Knight* remained stopped and burning all over. The master of the *O. B. Jennings*, realizing the danger, righted his helm and gave his ship a touch ahead with his engines and got clear of the dangerous area of burning oil on the water.

The New York Times' account of the collision continues:

> "We [*O. B. Jennings*] had our own safety to look after. The burning naphtha had poured out into the sea, and it would have been folly to launch lifeboats. It was then that [three of] the [escort] destroyers [*Garland*, *Oberon*, and *Pasley*] showed their resourcefulness, for they dashed through the burning oil, bumped alongside of us, and we jumped to their decks in safety. We lost only one man, a [merchant] seaman named Shea, who was either burned or fell overboard and drowned.
>
> ". . . The accident came at the close of a rough and exciting voyage, which had set the nerves of our crew on edge through the previously unaccounted-for disappearance of several ships of our convoy. They may have been diverted, or they may have been torpedoed. We never knew further than the fact that they were gone when we looked for them."

The rescue of all but one man on the *O. B. Jennings* was truly heroic on the part of the Royal Navy escort destroyers. The captain of the destroyer *Garland*, Lieutenant Edward Fegen,[29] was particularly resourceful and brave in the rescue effort. He and his helmsman were later awarded the Silver Medal for Gallantry for saving lives at sea. The citation for the award describes the scene when he encountered the *O. B. Jennings* and reads in part:

---

[29] Lt. Edward Fegen is the correct spelling of the name, as attested in his award citation, though spelled "Fegan" in the minutes of the *Court of Enquiry* papers.

The master of the *O. B. Jennings* gave orders that all the ship's available boats should be lowered, those on the starboard side were burnt, and the crew abandoned the ship in the port boats, whilst the Master, Chief Engineer, Chief Officer, and three others remained on board. HMS *Garland*, under the command of Lieutenant Fegen, with other destroyers, were proceeding to the spot to render assistance, when it was seen that one boat which had been lowered from the *O. B. Jennings* had been swamped. The *Garland* closed the *O. B. Jennings*, rescued the men from the swamped boat, and then proceeded alongside the ship, which was still blazing, and rescued those who were still on board. She afterwards proceeded to pick up the others who had left the ship in boats, rescuing in all four officers and twenty-two men.[30]

I must try to imagine where my father was just before the collision. He might have been on watch or possibly asleep in his bunk. I feel certain that wherever he was on the *O. B. Jennings* at the time of the collision, his training kicked in after many lifeboat drills, and he immediately reacted with all the other members of the crew to take to the lifeboats and abandon ship.

My father must have been on one of the lifeboats picked up by Lieutenant Fegen on the destroyer *Garland*, which then delivered the survivors to Victory Station in nearby Portsmouth. There the rescued seamen were cleaned up and given every consideration for their health and safety. They were all given fresh clothing, and in the case of the twenty-six US Navy armed guards, they were issued British RN uniforms until they would be back in US Navy supply channels. At some point after their rescue, a photo was taken of my father and two of the other Navy

---

[30] "Royal Navy & Merchant Navy Medals—Awards of the Albert Medal (AM) from *The London Gazette in Edition Order*," Naval-History.net, accessed May 30, 2025, https://naval-history.net/WW1NavyBritishLGDecorationszzAlbertMedal.htm.

Armed Guard survivors in RN uniforms. I believe I can detect a shade of relief and gratitude in their smiles.

Fig. 10. Photo of my father (center) wearing a loaned RN uniform following the collision

CHAPTER 10

— ★ —

The Collision As Experienced on the *War Knight*

Fig. 11. Photo of the War Knight *burning after collision with the O. B. Jennings (Courtesy of the National Maritime Museum and from the Dave Wendes collection)*[31]

---

[31] *Forgotten Wrecks, SS* War Knight *Site Report,* 9, https://maritimearchaeologytrust.org/wp-content/uploads/2021/01/FWFWW_WarKnight_SiteReport.pdf.

After the collision, the *War Knight* remained dead in the water consumed by fire. From all accounts, thirty-six of the forty-seven men on the *War Knight* were killed almost instantly from the fiery blast, which emerged from the pierced naphtha tanks on the *O. B. Jennings*. The resulting chaos was recorded in written statements by five of the eleven *War Knight* survivors after their miraculous rescue. Survivors included the ship's cook; the mess room steward; the 2nd cook (also known as the "pantry boy" or "greaser"); the chief engineer, 2nd engineer, 3rd engineer, 4th engineer, and 5th engineer; and the 3rd officer. These men were either off duty, sleeping in quarters below deck, or working in a place protected in some way from the initial blast that swept the main deck. The following are their transcribed original written statements, which detail the horror of the collision as they experienced it on the *War Knight*.

Leonard Mason, Mess Room Steward[32]

About 2.30 a.m. Sunday morning 24th March I was awakened by a violent jar. I got up and started to dress when I heard the signal for boat stations. I then went out of my room into the Port Alleyway to go to my station when I was surprised to see great tongues of flames sweeping over the deck from starboard.

I immediately rushed back and told my roommates (the 2nd Cook and Pantryboy) to get out of it at once as the ship was in flames. I tried to escape, but we were cut off from both doors. There was then great confusion in

---

[32] Leonard Mason, attached to letter from A. Dodsworth, Furness Withy & Co., Ltd. to Secretary of the Admiralty, Whitehall, May 30, 1918, published in *Court of Enquiry Order 0197/62 into Supposed Loss of US O. B. Jennings and War Knight, April 3–6, 1918*; UK National Archives, 537.

the Alleyway, several men were on fire with burning oil.

Thinking it too dangerous to remain any longer, I and the Chief Cook made our way through the galley into the Starboard Alleyway where we found equal confusion, the Alleyway being full of smoke. The first man I met was the Chief Engineer, who had rushed aft to get the fireman out. He was badly burnt about the face and hands. By this time the smoke and fumes were so thick we could see nothing and recognise nobody. The fumes, which I took to be naptha, were choking us.

The door at the fore part of the Alleyway was locked. I opened my pantry door and one of the Engineers took a large axe and tried to batten the door open, but was unable to. It was now impossible to breathe. I went into my pantry and soaked one of my white jackets in water and tied it around my mouth.

We were beginning to lose consciousness. I suggested breaking open the skylight, which I think was done, and I believe several escaped that way. I made my way to the after door for a final try to escape when the wind seemed to blow the flames away.

I got out on deck at last and saw the Chief, 3rd and 4th Engineers, the 3rd Officer and Apprentice Clayton, also a Greaser and the Cook. This was on the starboard side. We had to cross to the port side as the fire and smoke began to envelope us. We sighted a destroyer, and then jumped over the side. We were picked up later by a boat from the destroyer.

Whilst swimming to the boat I particularly noticed our bows telescoped in. At the same time I saw a man on the fore part of the ship waving his arms and shouting. Who he was I do not know. The Chief Engineer and 3rd Engineer were badly burnt, so also a Greaser.

I stumbled over several charred bodies on the deck. The boats appeared to have been burnt, one of which I saw floating away on fire. The whole of the bridge and cabin were in flames. We owe our lives I think to remaining in the Alleyway as the heat and flames on deck were terrific. It was impossible to keep our feet on the deck.

We were shown every kindness on board the destroyer, and landed at Portsmouth, where I and the Cook were fitted with clothes and sent to London.

```
                    S/S "WAR KNIGHT"                    537
          report made by Leonard Mason - Mess Room Steward.
          -------------------

          About 2.30 a.m. Sunday morning 24th March I was awakened
by a violent jar.    I got up and started to dress when I heard
the signal for boat stations.    I then went out of my room into
the Port Alleyway to go to my station when I was surprised to
see great tongues of flames sweeping over the deck from star-
board.    I immediately rushed back and told my room-mates
(the 2nd Cook and Pantryboy) to get out of it at once as the
ship was in flames.    I tried to escape, but we were cut off
from both doors.    There was then great confusion in the
Alleyway, several men were on fire with burning oil.    Think-
ing it too dangerous to remain any longer, I and the Chief Cook
made our way through the galley into the Starboard Alleyway
where we found equal confusion, the Alleyway being full of
smoke.    The first man I met was the Chief Engineer, who had
rushed aft to get the fireman out.    He was badly burnt about
the face and hands.    By this time the smoke and fumes were
so thick we could see nothing and recognise nobody.    The
fumes, which I took to be naptha, were choking us.    The
door at the fore part of the Alleyway was locked.    I opened
my pantry door and one of the Engineers took a large axe and
tried to batten the door open, but was unable to.    It was
now impossible to breathe.    I went into my pantry and soaked
one of my white jackets in water and tied it around my mouth.

          We were beginning to lose consciousness.    I suggested
breaking open the skylight, which I think was done, and I
believe several escaped that way.    I made my way to the
after door for a final try to escape when the wind seemed to
blow the flames away.

          I got out on deck at last and saw the Chief, 3rd and
4th Engineers, the 3rd Officer and Apprentice Clayton, also
a Greaser and the Cook.    This was on the starboard side.
We had to cross to the port side as the fire and smoke began
to envelope us.    We sighted a destroyer, and then jumped
over the side.    We were picked up later by a boat from the
destroyer.    Whilst swimming to the boat I particularly
noticed our bows telescoped in.    At the same time I saw a
man on the fore part of the ship waving his arms and shouting.
Who he was I do not know.    The Chief Engineer and 3rd
Engineer were badly burnt, so also a Greaser.

          I stumbled over several charred bodies on the deck.
The boats appeared to have been burnt, one of which I saw
floating away on fire.    The whole of the bridge and cabin
were in flames.    We owe our lives I think to remaining in
the Alleyway as the heat and flames on deck were terrific.
It was impossible to keep our feet on the deck.

          We were shown every kindness on board the destroyer,
and landed at Portsmouth, where I and the Cook were fitted
with clothes and sent to London.

                         (Signed) Leonard Mason.
                                  Mess Room Steward.
```

Fig. 12. Leonard Mason, O. B. Jennings–War Knight Court of Enquiry, p. 537

G. Heron, 2nd Engineer:[33]

At the time of the accident I was in my bed, having been there since 10 p.m. on the previous night. I was due on for duty again at 4 a.m. having charge of the 4 to 8 Watch. During this period in bed I was not once awake, and to my knowledge all was going well. In the event of anything happening in the Engine Room I would have been notified.

I was awakened by the concussion at a time I believe to be 2.30 a.m., although I did not see the actual time myself. I rose and partly dressed, and whilst doing so I had a visit from the Chief Engineer, who told me to dress with all haste but did not say anything as to what had happened. My first impulse was to see if the Turbine Engine had been stopped, which I ascertained on entering the Engine Room door.

By this time there was considerable heat and flame at the top of the Engine Room, and it was an impossibility to enter further. I returned to the Eng[ine] Alleyway on the star[board] side of the ship where I found several of the crew, but owing to the dense smoke and heat it was impossible to see who all were. There were several Engineers, and I have since learned from other accounts who most of these men were.

It appeared impossible to gain the deck from the aft end of the alleyway, so we attempted to open the door at the fore end, but to no avail, and due to this I think most of the men who were in the alleyway owe their escape, as had the door been opened, flames would have just reached from one end to the other.

I now decided there was little hope of salvation by

---

[33] G. Heron, attached to Dodsworth letter to Sec. of Admiralty, *Court of Enquiry*, 535–36.

remaining in the alleyway, so proceeded to the aft end again, where I wrapped an overcoat which I had with me over my face and hands and leaped through the flames over the ship's star[board] side. By the time I reached the water and came up again, the steamer with which we collided . . . was about, to my judgement, 2 ships' length away, and as far as I could judge was well in flames, at least on her port side, and our ship was one mass of flame from fore to aft.

The whole surface of the sea for some distance was one mass of burning oil, and I had great difficulty in keeping out of this oil owing to the wind or current drifting me on to it all the time. I saw no one in the water at any time, and could see no one on the ship, only hear a number of pitiful cries from time to time.

There was nothing to see of the rest of the convoy, at least from my position, for at least half an hour from the time I took to the water until I then sighted two of our Torpedo boats coming in my direction. I "halloed" and after a period during which I thought they were going to pass me, I was at last sighted by one of the Commanders, who picked me up.

By this time I would be at least a quarter of a mile from the ship (my ship), and she did not appear to be burning so fiercely then; most of the oil on the water had burnt out by this time also.

I was taken on board the Torpedo boat, and shown every care, but I was not in a serious condition in any way and soon got over my immersion in the water. I was not burnt sufficiently in any way to warrant any medical attention.

I saw there were a number of survivors of the *O. B. Jennings* but saw none of our men at the time. I was taken by the First Lieutenant down the ward room where I was clothed with dry gear. I then went up on deck and found there were four survivors in all from the *War Knight* viz:- Mr. Brown, 3rd Officer, Apprentice Clayton, and A. B. Howe, the two latter being seriously burnt.

We were then cruising around in the vain hope of picking up any more survivors, but when well on to daybreak, our Commander decided there were little or no hopes of other rescues and proceeded to Portsmouth to obtain better medical attention for the two badly burnt men.

We were landed about 9 a.m. and proceeded to the Speedwell Temperance Hotel, where I ascertained from the 4th Engineer, Mr. Hill, and 5th, Mr. Broatch, that there were only 11 survivors in all of *War Knight*. Five of these are badly burned and in hospital at Portsmouth.

I have been there to see them all of course, and both the Chief Engineer and Apprentice Clayton who can perhaps give some better account, as they were on or about the decks at the time, are in too bad a condition to give me any account.

The 3rd Engineer merely states that he had several movements on the engines previous to the collision in the order, as far as I know, from the Standing Full ahead to Slow Ahead and then Full Astern and afterwards abandon ship. He shut everything up on the Turbine and put out all the fires on the oil fuel boilers and had great difficulty due to heat and flames entering the Engine Room from gaining the deck, during which time both he and his fireman were badly burnt.

(Signed) G. Heron

535

S/S "WAR KNIGHT"

Report made by G. Heron, 2nd Engineer.

At the time of the accident I was in my bed, having been there since 10 p.m. on the previous night. I was due on for duty again at 4 a.m. having charge of the 4 to 8 Watch. During this period in bed I was not once awake, and to my knowledge all was going well. In the event of anything happening in the Engine Room I would have been notified.

I was awakened by the concussion at a time I believe to be 2.30 a.m., although I did not see the actual time myself. I rose and partly dressed, and whilst doing so I had a visit from the Chief Engineer, who told me to dress with all haste, but did not say anything as to what had happened. My first impulse was to see if the Turbine Engine had been stopped, which I ascertained on entering the Engine Room door. By this time there was considerable heat and flame at the top of the Engine Room, and it was an impossibility to enter further. I returned to the Eng: Alleyway on the star side of the ship where I found several of the crew, but owing to the dense smoke and heat it was impossible to see who all were. There were several Engineers, and I have since learned from other accounts who most of these men were. It appeared impossible to gain the deck from the aft end of the alleyway, so we attempted to open the door at the fore end, but to no avail, and due to this I think most of the men who were in the alleyway owe their escape, as had the door been opened flames would have just reached from one end to the other. I now decided there was little hope of salvation by remaining in the alleyway, so proceeded to the aft end again, where I wrapped an overcoat which I had with me over my face and hands and leaped through the flames over the ship's star side. By the time I reached the water and came up again, the steamer with which we collided if it were a collision, which proved to be afterwards the O.B. Jennings of New York, an Oil Tank loaded mainly with Naptha, was about, to my judgment, 2 ships' length away, and as far as I could judge was well in flames, at least on her Port side, and our ship was one mass of flame from fore to aft. The whole surface of the sea for some distance was one mass of burning oil, and I had great difficulty in keeping out of this oil owing to the wind or current drifting me on to it all the time. I saw no one in the water at any time, and could see no one on the ship, only hear a number of pitiful cries from time to time. There was nothing to see of the rest of the convoy, at least from my position, for at least half an hour from the time I took to the water, until I then sighted two of our Torpedo boats coming in my direction. I "hallooed" and after a period during which I thought they were going to pass me, I was at last sighted by one of the Commanders, who picked me up. By this time I would be at least a quarter of a mile from the ship (my ship) and she did not appear to be burning so fiercely then, most of the oil on the water had burnt out by this time also. I was taken on board the Torpedo boat, and shewn every care, but I was not in a serious condition in any way, and soon got over my immersion in the water. I was not burnt sufficiently in any way to warrant any medical attention. I saw there were a number of survivors of the O.B. Jennings, but saw none of our men at the time. I was taken by the First Lieutenant down the Ward Room

Fig. 13. 2nd Engineer Heron, O. B. Jennings–War Knight Court of Enquiry, p. 535

```
                              ( 2 )                          536


     where I was clothed with dry gear.     I then went up on
     deck and found there were four survivors in all from the
     "WAR KNIGHT" viz:- Mr.Brown, 3rd Officer, Apprentice
     Clayton and A.B.Howe, the two latter being seriously
     burnt.   We were then cruising around in the vain hope of
     picking up any more survivors, but when well on to daybreak
     our Commander decided there were little or no hopes of
     other rescues, and proceeded to Portsmouth to obtain better
     medical attention for the two badly burnt men.

              We were landed about 9 a.m. and proceeded to the
     Speedwell Temperance Hotel, where I ascertained from the
     4th Engineer Mr.Hill and 5th Mr.Broatch that there were
     only 11 survivors in all off "WAR KNIGHT".    Five of
     these are badly burned and in Hospital at Portsmouth.

              I have been there to see them all of course, and
     both the Chief Engineer and Apprentice Clayton who can
     perhaps give some better account, as they were on or about
     the decks at the time, are in too bad a condition to give
     me any account.

              The 3rd Engineer merely states that he had several
     movements on the engines previous to the collision in the
     order, as far as I know, from the Standing Full ahead to
     Slow Ahead and then Full Astern and afterwards abandon ship.
     He shut everything up on the Turbine and put out all the
     fires on the oil fuel boilers and had great difficulty
     due to heat and flames entering the Engine Room from gain-
     ing the deck, during which time both he and his fireman were
     badly burnt.


                              (Signed) G. Heron.
```

Fig. 14. 2nd Engineer Heron, O. B. Jennings—War Knight Court of Enquiry, p. 536

George Brown, 3rd Officer:[34]

I have to report that the SS *War Knight* left Philadelphia on Tuesday the 5th of March and New York sailing in convoy on Friday the [22nd] of March, arriving in the Channel on Saturday morning the 23rd of March.

---

[34] George Brown, attached to Dodsworth letter to Sec. of Admiralty, *Court of Enquiry*, 534.

On the night of the accident I was on the bridge from 8 p.m. till 12 midnight. At 11 p.m. the Captain went below, leaving instructions to inform 2nd officer when he relieved me at midnight to call him at 2 a.m., as several ships were then to leave the convoy for Spithead, and that, if he should see any ships leaving before that time, to inform him at once.

On being relieved by the 2nd Officer I passed these instructions on to him, and then went below, the ship at that time being on her proper station.

About 2.30 a.m. I was awakened by a violent impact. Jumping out of my bunk, I rushed to the door and looked out on deck, and found the whole ship to be in flames. At this time I heard the signal on the Engine Room telegraph to abandon the Engine Room, and the signal given on the steam whistle for all hands to take to the boats. Turning back to my room to put on a few clothes I observed Captain Holroyd hurrying past in the direction of the boats and at the same time the Chief Officer rushed out of his room and made in the same direction.

I followed on as soon as possible, the ship then being one mass of flames from stem to stern. On arriving on the boat deck I found that both lifeboats had been burned away.

The boat deck being unbearable with smoke and flames I hurried over the after end of the boat deck and took shelter in the Engineer's alleyway where I found the 2nd, 3rd, 4th, and 5th Engineers, one fireman, Messroom Steward and Chief Cook. After a few minutes the alleyway became unbearable from flames and smoke. Ultimately we burst open the Engineers Messroom skylight and came through again on to the boat deck which by this time had partly cleared.

We got to the after end of the ship weather side where we met the Chief Engineer and Apprentice Clayton. After some time we were hailed by a destroyer and told to jump into the water, as it was too dangerous for him to approach closer. We did this, and were taken on board the destroyer, where we were treated with great kindness. From the deck of the destroyer I observed a sailor named Howe on the fore deck, he was taken off by a boat from another destroyer. I am sure that no other living person was left aboard the ship. I was landed at Portsmouth and put up at the Speedwell Hotel and on Wednesday came to London and reported myself at the Office.

(Signed) George Brown
3rd Officer

```
                                        FURNESS, WITHY & Co., LTD.
                                              FURNESS HOUSE
                                              BILLITER S[...]    534
                                              LONDON, E.C. 3.

        S/S "W A R   K N I G H T"

              Report made by George Brown 3rd Officer.
                      30th March 1918.


         I have to report that the S/S "WAR KNIGHT" left
    Philadelphia on Tuesday the 5th of March and New York
    sailing in convoy on Friday the 28th of March, arriving in
    the Channel on Saturday morning the 23rd of March.

         On the night of the accident I was on the bridge from
    8 p.m. till 12 midnight.   At 11 p.m. the Captain went
    below, leaving instructions to inform 2nd Officer when he
    relieved me at midnight to call him at 2 a.m., as several
    ships were then to leave the convoy for Spithead, and that,
    if he should see any ships leaving before that time, to
    inform him at once.

         On being relieved by the 2nd Officer I passed these
    instructions on to him, and then went below, the ship at
    that time being on her proper station.

         About 2.30 a.m. I was awakened by a violent impact.
    Jumping out of my bunk, I rushed to the door and looked out
    on deck, and found the whole ship to be in flames.   At
    this time I heard the signal on the Engine Room telegraph to
    abandon the Engine Room, and the signal given on the steam
    whistle for all hands to take to the boats.   Turning back
    to my room to put on a few clothes I observed Captain Hol-
    royd hurrying past in the direction of the boats and at the
    same time the Chief Officer rushed out of his room and made
    in the same direction.

         I followed on as soon as possible, the ship then being
    one mass of flames from stem to stern.   On arriving on the
    boat deck I found that both lifeboats had been burned away.

         The boat deck being unbearable with smoke and flames
    I hurried over the after end of the boat deck and took
    shelter in the Engineer's alleyway where I found the 2nd,
    3rd, 4th and 5th Engineers, one fireman, Messroom Steward
    and Chief Cook.   After a few minutes the alleyway became
    unbearable from flames and smoke.   Ultimately we burst
    open the Engineers Messroom skylight and came through again
    on to the boat deck which by this time had partly cleared.

         We got to the after end of the ship weather side where
    we met the Chief Engineer and Apprentice Clayton.

         After some time we were hailed by a destroyer and told
    to jump into the water, as it was too dangerous for him to
    approach closer.   We did this, and were taken on board
    the destroyer, where we were treated with great kindness.

         From the deck of the destroyer I observed a sailor named
    Howe on the fore deck, he was taken off by a boat from another
    destroyer.   I am sure that no other living person was left
    aboard the ship.

         I was landed at Portsmouth and put up at the Speedwell
    Hotel and on Wednesday came to London and reported myself
    at the Office.
                         (Signed) GEORGE BROWN.
                                     3rd Officer.
```

Fig. 15. 3rd Officer George Brown, O. B. Jennings—War Knight Court of Enquiry, p. 534

T. Barker, 3rd Engineer[35]

On March 24th at 2.20 a.m., when a collision occurred between S/S *War Knight* and S/S *O. B. Jennings* which caused both ships to take fire, I was on watch in the engine room. Immediately after the collision I saw flames sweeping across the top of the engine room through the open skylight. Mr. Falconer the Chief Engineer stood in the flames and shut the skylights down to prevent them entering the engine room.

I remained at the throttle working the engines as ordered by telegraph for about 10 minutes after the collision, and getting no reply from the bridge, I shut off oil-fuel and fires, stopped engines which had been ordered half-speed ahead by last order, and made my way on deck with Wishart the fireman who had stayed below with me. The engine room was then filling with fumes. I stepped into the port alleyway and was severely burned by a rush of flame and gassed by fumes.

Mr. Falconer came across the engine-room platform and dragged me and Wishart across to the starboard alleyway where there was less flames and fumes. He then put us into the engineers' messroom with others that he had collected from their bunks. He broke open the skylight of the messroom and assisted each one to get on to the boat deck.

As I was semi-conscious and the deck very hot, Mr. Falconer held me in his arms. A destroyer's boat then came as near as it could get owing to the heat. I told Mr. Falconer to look out for himself, but he said he would see me alright first. I had not a lifebelt on, so he took his off and put it on me and dropped me over the side, and he remained on the deck.

---

[35] T. Barker, attached to Dodsworth letter to Sec. of Admiralty, *Court of Enquiry*, 540–41.

After satisfying himself that there were no others in need of assistance, he jumped into the water and was some time struggling to reach the boat, as he could not swim. He collapsed on board the destroyer and was taken to the Portsmouth Royal Hospital, where he died on April 6th from injuries to his lungs.

I consider his action undoubtedly saved my life and that of Wishart the fireman, and also the lives of the remaining survivors, particularly the 2nd Engineer, 4th Engineer, 5th Engineer, Chief Cook, and Messroom boy. These people he had roused out of their bunks and assisted in every way possible.

Mr. Barker's statement.

On March 24th at 2.20 a.m. when a collision occurred between S/S "WAR KNIGHT" and S/S "O.B.JENNINGS" which caused both ships to take fire, I was on watch in the engine room. Immediately after the collision I saw flames sweeping across the top of the engine room through the open skylight. Mr.Falconer the Chief Engineer stood in the flames and shut the skylights down to prevent them entering the engine room. I remained at the throttle working the engines as ordered by telegraph for about 10 minutes after the collision, and getting no reply from the bridge I shut off oil-fuel and fires, stopped engines which had been ordered half-speed ahead by last order, and made my way on deck with Wishart the fireman who had stayed below with me. The engine room was then filling with fumes. I stepped into the Port alleyway and was severely burned by a rush of flame, and gassed by fumes. Mr.Falconer came across the engine-room platform and dragged me and Wishart across to the starboard alleyway where there was less flames and fumes. He then put us into the Engineers' messroom with others that he had collected from their bunks. He broke open the skylight of the messroom and assisted each one to get on to the boat deck. As I was semi-conscious and the deck very hot, Mr.Falconer held me in his arms. A destroyer's boat then came as near as it could get owing to the heat. I told Mr.Falconer to look out for himself, but he said he would see me alright first. I had not a lifebelt on, so he took his off and put it on me and dropped me over the side and he remained on the deck. After satisfying himself that there were no others in need of assistance he jumped into the water and was some time struggling to reach the boat, as he could not swim. He collapsed on board the destroyer, and was taken to the Portsmouth Royal Hospital, where he died on April 6th from injuries to his lungs.

I consider his action undoubtedly saved my life and that of

Fig. 16. 3rd Engineer Barker, O. B. Jennings–War Knight Court of Enquiry, p. 540

```
                (2)                                           541

Wishart the fireman, and also the lives of the remaining survivors
particularly the 2nd Engineer, 4th Engineer, 5th Engineer, Chief
Cook, and Messroom boy.   These people he had roused out of their
bunks and assisted in every way possible.

                        (Signed) T. BARKER.
                                 3rd Engineer.
```

Fig. 17. 3rd Engineer Barker, O. B. Jennings–War Knight Court of Enquiry, p. 541

F. Hagerty, Ship's Cook:[36]

26th March 1918

We left New York on being one of a convoy of 35 ships escorted by an American Cruiser. All went well until Sunday morning 24th March. I retired about 12.30 on Saturday night, and at 2.50 I was awakened by a jarring sound.

Thinking we had been torpedoed I slipped out of bed, pulled on my working trousers and a singlet, I threw my shore coat and trousers over my arm, and put on a lifebelt. In about a minute I was out in the alleyway. This was already a mass of flames and smoke. One or two men were rushing about on fire. One of them brushed against the Steward's boy and, I think, set him on fire.

In company with a man who proved to be Mason, I rushed through the galley into the starboard alleyway. This was also full of smoke, which I think was really gas, generated by the naptha. In this alleyway were

---

[36] F. Hagarty, attached to Dodsworth letter to Sec. of Admiralty, *Court of Enquiry*, 538–539.

gathered all the men who, up to now, are the only survivors. One or two went down overcome by the fumes; I heard them moaning.

I can't say how the other men saved their lives: this is how I saved mine. I had got a cloth somewhere, and had it over my mouth and nose, but it was of very little avail. I went down but managed to get up again. I staggered into somewhere which proved to be a lavatory. Several men were here also suffocating like myself. Someone had an axe, and attacked the alleyway door, but it was no good.

I went down again, as I thought for good. I could not breathe. As I fell my hand caught something which proved to be a flush lavatory. I pushed my face in here and threw salt water over it. I am positive this saved my life. I gasped out "water boys" and the other fellows who heard me did the same. We were all pretty nearly mad about now: some made a rush and got through some skylight or something on to the boat deck.

I rushed along the alleyway and got out on deck. The wind, or else the ship bearing round, had blown the flames over to the port side. All the men who were landed safely seem[ed] to have made their escape at that time out of the alleyway. I was the last man to get out, and I found them all on deck. The flames swept over to the starboard side again in a few seconds, so we ran across to the port side; it was red hot here. We put our feet over the rails and shouted as loudly as possible, and in a few minutes a Destroyer came up and lowered a boat.

We jumped into the water and were picked up. The Destroyer landed us at Portsmouth at about 6.30 on Sunday morning. The Chief Engineer, 3rd Engineer, and 1 Greaser were admitted to the Hospital badly burnt.

Not more than 20 minutes could have elapsed from

the collision until we were picked up by the Destroyer. The ship was a roaring furnace in about 2 minutes.

When we got on deck we saw a lifeboat in the water just a piece of charcoal. One of the survivors said he saw four dead bodies on the boat deck; he could not recognise them.

The *War Knight*'s bow was badly damaged. I think she hit the *O. B. Jennings* nearly aft.

The men saved with myself were:
Leonard Mason
Chief Engineer
2nd Engineer
3rd Engineer
4th Engineer
5th Engineer
3rd Officer
1 Greaser

According to my reckoning there was about 47 of crew.

(S'd) F. Hagarty
Ship's Cook

Report made by F. Hagarty - Ship's Cook -
S/S "WAR KNIGHT"

26th March 1918.

We left New York on   being one of a convoy of 35 ships escorted by an American Cruiser. All went well until Sunday morning 24th March. I retired about 12.30 on Saturday night, and at 2.50 I was awakened by a jarring sound. Thinking we had been torpedoed I slipped out of bed, pulled on my working trousers and a singlet, I threw my shore coat and trousers over my arm, and put on a lifebelt. In about a minute I was out in the alleyway. This was already a mass of flames and smoke. One or two men were rushing about on fire. One of them brushed against the Steward's boy and, I think, set him on fire. In company with a man who proved to be Mason, I rushed through the galley into the starboard alleyway. This was also full of smoke, which I think was really gas, generated by the Naptha. In this alleyway were gathered all the men who, up to now, are the only survivors. One or two went down overcome by the fumes, I heard them moaning. I can't say how the other men saved their lives; this is how I saved mine. I had got a cloth somewhere, and had it over my mouth and nose, but it was of very little avail. I went down but managed to get up again. I staggered into somewhere which proved to be a lavatory. Several men were here also suffocating like myself. Someone had an axe, and attacked the alleyway door, but it was no good. I went down again, as I thought for good. I could not breathe. As I fell my hand caught something which proved to be a flush lavatory. I pushed my face in here and threw salt water over it. I am positive this saved my life. I gasped out "water boys" and the other fellows who heard me did the same. We were all pretty nearly mad about now: some made a rush and got through

Fig. 18. F. Hagarty, O. B. Jennings–War Knight Court of Enquiry, p. 538

(2)

some skylight or something on to the boat deck. I rushed along the alleyway and got out on deck. The wind, or else the ship bearing round, had blown the flames over to the port side. All the men who were landed safely seem to have made their escape at that time out of the alleyway. I was the last man to get out, and I found them all on deck. The flames swept over to the starboard side again in a few seconds so we ran across to the port side: it was red hot here: we put our feet over the rails and shouted as loudly as possible, and in a few minutes a Destroyer came up and lowered a boat. We jumped into the water and were picked up. The Destroyer landed us at Portsmouth at about 6.30 on Sunday morning. The Chief Engineer, 3rd Engineer and 1 Greaser were admitted to the Hospital badly burnt.

Not more than 20 minutes could have elapsed from the collision until we were picked up by the Destroyer.

The ship was a roaring furnace in about 2 minutes.

When we got on deck we saw a lifeboat in the water just a piece of charcoal.

One of the survivors said he saw four dead bodies on the boat deck, he could not recognise them.

The War Knight's bow was badly damaged. I think she hit the "O.B.Jennings" nearly aft.

The men saved with myself were :-

    Leonard Mason
    Chief Engineer
    2nd Engineer
    3rd Engineer
    4th Engineer
    5th Engineer
    3rd Officer
    1 Greaser

According to my reckoning there was about 47 of crew.

(S'd) F. HAGARTY.
Ship's Cook.

Fig. 19. F. Hagarty, O. B. Jennings–War Knight *Court of Enquiry Report*, p. 539

Noteworthy in the above accounts of the collision are the heroic actions of the chief engineer, Mr. David Falconer. He later died from burns and smoke inhalation and was awarded a Silver Medal for gallantry.

THE COLLISION AS SEEN BY THE ENEMY

The submarine threat that caused Convoy HN53B to make such a wide course alteration turned out to be very real. German submarine *UB-59*, a Type III coastal boat commanded by Kapitanleutnant zur See Erwin Wassner, was on patrol on the nights of March 23 and 24, 1918, in the vicinity of the collision.[37] Ironically, Wassner was remarkably well placed to witness and validate this terrible disaster. In the U-boat KTB (war diary), Wassner wrote:

> 3am. Heard in our immediate vicinity and repeatedly, the sound of a whistle. Carefully turned toward the sound. Visibility poor.
>
> 3.50am. There is a big explosion, with a high, blood red sheet of flame which grew higher and higher, and spread out in all directions. We were able to see two steamers, and both were in a blaze of fire, and several destroyers and steamers moved past them. According to radio messages which we overheard, a collision had taken place. Apparently, one of the steamers was a tanker. For hours it was possible to see two large burning spots on the water.

---

[37] David Wendes, *South Coast Shipwrecks off East Dorset & Wight 1870–1979* (Chandler's Ford, UK, 2006), 183–184.

Although the timings logged by Wassner in his war diary do not match exactly the actual times of the collision events, the remainder of his account clearly describes the collision scene. There is no hiding a catastrophe of this magnitude on the open sea.

To further validate Wassner's account, the "two explosions and a flash of light" observed some miles off by Commander Blackwood on the *Syringa* at 12:30 a.m. were probably an action in which the *UB-59* had been earlier engaged also recorded in Wassner's war diary. While Wassner was not able to fire his torpedoes directly at the ships in Convoy HN53B, his reporting indicates that his U-boat was clearly a player in shaping the drama that night.

CHAPTER 11

---★---

The Immediate Aftermath of the Collision

Despite the hellish scene of two ships and the water surrounding them engulfed in fire, the destroyers *Garland*, *Oberon*, and *Pasley* conducted heroic rescues of all but one member of the *O. B. Jennings* crew and eleven of the forty-seven-man crew of *War Knight*. They were helped by an armed trawler and several patrol boats and motor launches that arrived on the scene.

Convoy HN53B continued on course despite its broken order and disarray until daylight. The merchant ship *Mirlo*, which was next to the *O. B. Jennings* at the time of the collision, bolted from the collision scene, departed the convoy, and headed for Portland, its nearby port of destination. The master of the *Mirlo* informed no one of his actions, and the SEO had to initially report the ship missing until it was sighted at berth in Portland. Such action demonstrated the lack of discipline and the vagueness of standing orders that took place as the convoy system was evolving.

The destroyers were able to attach a towline on the blazing *War Knight* and began to tow her toward the shallow waters and beach her on the Isle of Wight just a few miles away. During the tow, the unfortunate *War Knight* drifted into a minefield placed there the day before by a German submarine. Two mines exploded beneath the *War Knight,* and a third contacted the towing wire. The vessel was then stranded in Watcombe Bay near the town of Freshwater off the Isle of Wight and eventually scuttled by gunfire to extinguish the fires.

The destroyers on the scene also made the decision that the burning *O. B. Jennings* would be a menace to other ships in the busy shipping lanes off the Isle of Wight, and they scuttled her with a number of shots fired into her hold. She settled in the water until her decks were level with the surface, which extinguished the flames. Afterward, she was taken in tow and beached off the Isle of Wight with the hope and intention that she could be refloated and repaired.

CHAPTER 12

Accountability for the Collision

I was initially disappointed and concerned that my thorough search for information on the collision of the *O. B. Jennings* and *War Knight* from official US Navy sources disclosed no results. It then occurred to me that except for the twenty-six Navy armed guards on the *O. B. Jennings*, the US Navy was only minimally involved. Since all the armed guards survived the collision and were not involved in any aspect of the collision, the US Navy had no accountability. They eventually assumed responsibility for the US Navy men at Victory Station, Portsmouth, where they had been delivered by the destroyers after the collision.

My father and his armed guard mates stayed at Victory Station for thirty-three days. Once back in US Navy channels, the men were returned for reassignment to the US aboard the SS *New York* which departed Liverpool on April 26, 1918, and arrived at the Brooklyn Navy Yard, New York, on May 7, 1918. I have the ship manifest of the SS *New York* listing my father's name.

The British, on the other hand, took proper and full responsibility for investigating the collision since it took place under their escort protection and in their waters. Parties interested and concerned with accountability included the Royal Navy, the owners of the *War Knight* and *O. B. Jennings*, their insurance companies, and the British shipping controller, who had operational control of the *War Knight* at the time of the collision. Within days, the investigation began to determine accountability for the collision.

The commander in chief of HM Ships and Vessels, Plymouth, had the convening authority to establish an Admiralty Court of Enquiry, and by March 28, it must have become quite apparent to him from the information in the initial reports he was receiving that a formal inquiry was needed to investigate the collision of the *O. B. Jennings* and *War Knight*.

Accordingly, the commander in chief of HM Ships and Vessels issued order 0197/62, dated March 28, 1918, "to enquire into the circumstances attending the collision which occurred between the oilers *O. B. Jennings* and *War Knight*, whilst in convoy HN53, on the night of 23/24 March 1918."[38] This order set in motion the formal proceedings for a court of inquiry. Two senior Royal Navy officers, Flag Captain Cecil H. Fox, RN (president), and Commander Morshead B. Baillie-Hamilton, RN HMS *Apollo*, were assigned this duty.[39]

SUMMARY AND HIGHLIGHTS OF ADMIRALTY COURT OF ENQUIRY

The court was held aboard HMS *Eclipse* (command ship of Captain D, 4th Flotilla) on April 3 and continued on April 4 and 6, 1918. These proceedings were being done under wartime

---

[38] *Court of Enquiry Order 0197/62*, 475.
[39] The original Admiralty file obtained from the UK National Archives is available at joetedeschi.com for interested readers. The file contains all the official papers developed as a result of the investigation, which includes the report of the Admiralty Court of Enquiry with supporting documents, correspondence forwarding the report for review and approval by higher authorities, correspondence concerning cause and accountability for the collision, and recognition of valorous actions. A spreadsheet describing each page of the file is also provided for easy reference. https://joetedeschi.com/uk-natl-archives-court-of-enquiry/

conditions as evidenced by the hastily prepared handwritten reports initially made by key eyewitnesses. I can only imagine the difficulties of assembling key eyewitnesses, most of whom were then actively engaged in urgent ongoing naval operations. The court of enquiry was conducted in a formal manner reminiscent of the court martial scene in the movie *The Caine Mutiny*. Witnesses were called and sworn in, and their testimony was formally transcribed for the record. The handwritten reports of the collision hastily prepared soon after the collision were entered into the court record of proceedings.

As the SEO of the convoy, Commander Blackwood's two initial handwritten accounts were closely reviewed and scrutinized by the court. His accounts included two important attachments. The first (labeled "Schedule A") was a sketch of the events with the courses and times of alteration of courses (a/c) of Convoy HN53B on March 23 and 24, 1918. The second attachment (labeled "Schedule B") shows the formation of the merchant ships and the position of escort ships.

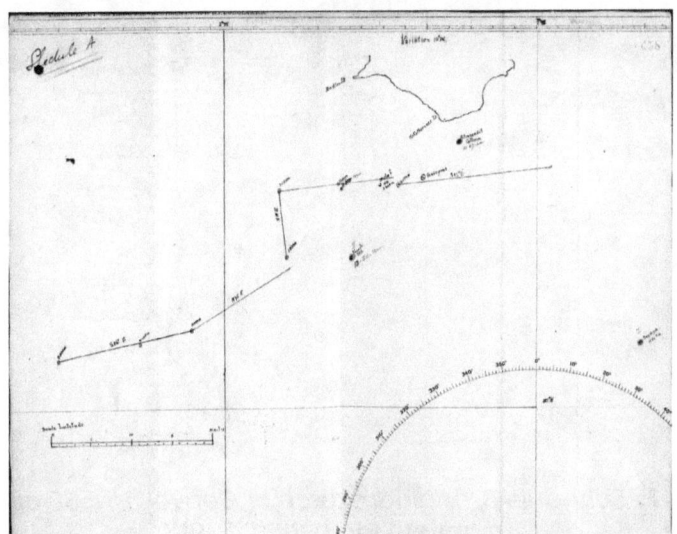

Fig. 20. Schedule A, original sketch of the events and courses and times of alteration of courses of Convoy HN53B on March 23–24, 1918, Court of Enquiry, p. 458

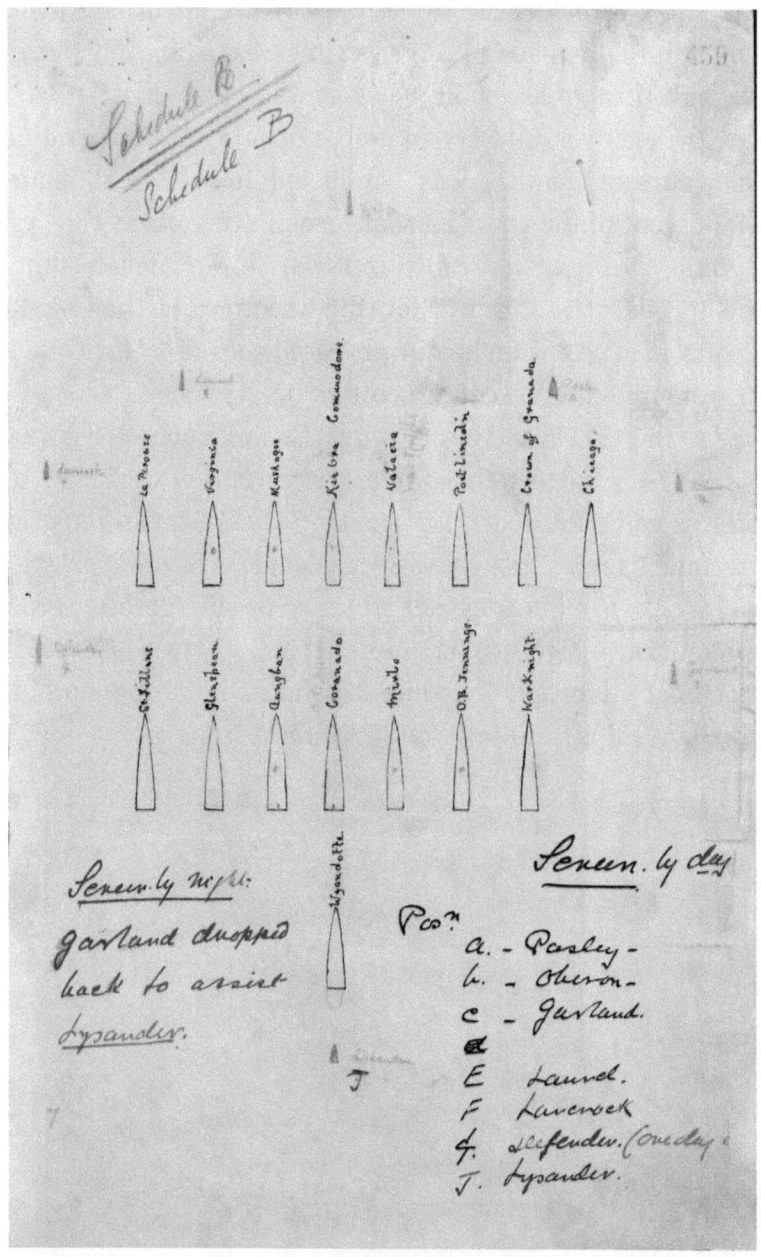

Fig. 21. Schedule B, original sketch of Convoy HN53B on the night of March 23–24, 1918 (Escort RN ships marked lightly in pencil), Court of Enquiry, p. 459

The convoy sketch lists the following sixteen merchant ships:

1. *La Perouse*
2. *Virginia*
3. *Muskagee*
4. *Kia Ora (Commodore)*
5. *Valacia*
6. *Port Lincoln*
7. *Crown of Grenada*
8. *Chicago*
9. *St. Fillans*
10. *Glenspean*
11. *Aungban*
12. *Coronado*
13. *Mirlo*
14. *O. B. Jennings*
15. *War Knight*
16. *Wyandotte*

Additionally, it also shows the SEO's ship, *Syringa*, leading the convoy and the lettered screening positions of the other Royal Navy escort destroyers by day, and at night the *Garland* dropped back in the convoy to assist the *Lysander*.

A. *Pasley*
B. *Oberon*

C. *Garland*

E. *Laurel*

F. *Laverock*

G. *Defender* (departed the convoy at midnight, March 23)

J. *Lysander*

Sworn testimony to the court by the destroyers' commanders as key eyewitnesses on the scene was supported and augmented by their handwritten reports of the collision. The master of the *O. B. Jennings*, George W. Nordston, also gave sworn testimony before the court.

FINDINGS OF THE COURT OF ENQUIRY

After deliberation, the court summarized their findings on April 6 and forwarded their report for consideration by higher authorities. Their conclusions (directly quoted below) were:

A. The collision between the *War Knight* and the *O. B. Jennings* was due to the former vessel altering course to starboard on sighting the port bow light of the *Aungban*. We consider that the theory put forward by the commanding officer of the *O. B. Jennings*, viz., that the steering gear of the *War Knight* had got out of control, although possible, was not probable.

B. The circumstances which led up to the collision were mainly due to some of the vessels in the convoy not having received the signals to alter course to NNE and S 82 E.

C. The commanding officer of HMS *Syringa* was justified

in altering the course of the convoy on both occasions, but he did not fully recognize the length of time it takes all the vessels of the convoy to receive signals when using the procedure he did, and that, had he acted with more promptitude on hearing the explosions and sighting the flare at 0030, the necessity for such large alterations of course would not have arisen, and, to this extent, we consider he is to blame.

D. Under the circumstances, the commanding officer of the *Syringa* was justified in detaching the Spithead portion of the convoy when he did.

E. Under the circumstances, the wireless signaling by *Syringa* was not excessive, and her commanding officer was justified in making the wireless signals he did.

F. There was submarine activity in that portion of the English Channel on the night of 23/24th.

G. The rescue work carried out by the destroyers was creditable, more especially that done by HMS *Garland*, great credit being due to Lieutenant Edward S.F. [Fegen], RN, for the able manner in which he handled his ship under difficult conditions. [40]

The report was processed through channels to the UK Admiralty for final disposition. After further careful deliberations, they determined blame for the collision and corrective actions to be taken, notified the proper authority to recognize valorous actions, and reported the basis for insurance company claims.

---

[40] *Court of Enquiry Order 0197/62*, 473–474.

BLAME AND CORRECTIVE ACTIONS

In line with the nature of all hierarchical military organizations, blame had to be fixed, and Commander Blackwood, SEO of Convoy HN53B, was singled out for blame for the collision of the *O. B. Jennings* and *War Knight*. While most of his actions and decisions were deemed justified, blame was assigned due to his failure to recognize the length of time it took to pass communications of course changes within the convoy.

It can only be hoped that Commander Blackwood's Royal Navy career was not tarnished by being singled out for blame this way. There were just too many loose ends and chances for error that night, and it is testimony to the seamanship and professionalism of all those who operated under the convoy system that more of these catastrophes did not occur.

The report was also useful in providing critical wisdom for all those daily involved in the ongoing convoy system. Prompt instructions were issued by the UK Admiralty to correct the deficiencies that were revealed by this convoy collision.

RECOGNITION OF VALOROUS ACTIONS

While there were many heroic actions taken by the Royal Navy and the merchant seamen throughout the collision and the immediate aftermath, four individuals (two RN and two merchant service) were specifically recognized in the report for valorous actions. The report made note of these actions, and in the ensuing correspondence, the proper authorities and channels for recognition were notified to issue appropriate awards.

On March 18, 1919, the two RN individuals were formally recognized and awarded medals. The award citation reads:

> His Majesty, the King is pleased, on the recommendation

of the President of the Board of Trade, to award the Silver Medal for gallantry in saving life at sea to Lieutenant Edward Stephen Fogarty Fegen, R.N. and Chief Petty Officer Patrick Driscoll, R.N.

On the 24th March 1918, while the British HMS *War Knight* was proceeding up the English Channel in convoy, she collided with the United States oil carrier *O. B. Jennings*. It appears that the naphtha, which was on board the latter vessel, ignited and the two ships and the surrounding water were soon enveloped in flames. The Master of the *O. B. Jennings* gave orders that all the ship's available boats should be lowered, those on the starboard side were burnt, and the crew abandoned the ship in the port boats, whilst the Master, Chief Engineer, Chief Officer and three others remained on board. HMS *Garland*, under the command of Lieutenant Fegen, with other destroyers, were proceeding to the spot to render assistance, when it was seen that one boat which had been lowered from the *O. B. Jennings* had been swamped. The *Garland* closed the *O. B. Jennings*, rescued the men from the swamped boat, and then proceeded alongside the ship, which was still blazing, and rescued those who were still on board. She afterwards proceeded to pick up the others who had left the ship in boats, rescuing in all four officers and twenty-two men. Lieutenant Fegen handled his ship in a very able manner under difficult conditions during the rescue of the survivors, while Driscoll worked the helm and saw that all orders to the engine-room were correctly carried out. [41]

Lieutenant Fegen's gallant naval career did not end with

---

[41] "Royal Navy & Merchant Navy Medals—Awards of the Albert Medal," Naval-History.net.

World War I.[42] He was killed in action during World War II and received the Victoria Cross for his actions while escorting ships of Convoy HX-84. While SEO of the convoy and commanding the armed cruiser *Jervis Bay*, Captain Fegen exhibited incredible courage and bravery in performing his escort duties, which saved the convoy from disastrous losses.

In the open sea of the Atlantic Ocean on November 5, 1940, Convoy HX-84 was attacked by the German battleship *Admiral Scheer*. Captain Fegen immediately steamed to engage the enemy head-on, to give the ships of the convoy time to scatter. Outgunned and on fire, the HMS *Jervis Bay* maintained the unequal fight for three hours with the German battleship. Although Captain Fegen's right arm was shattered and the bridge of his ship was shot from under him, he continued to fight until he went down with his ship. Due to the effort of Captain Fegen and his crew, the convoy was able to escape with only a few ships lost.

This incredible man and hero also saved my father from the burning sea. What award or level of homage can I ever give him?

Two of the civilian merchant-service seamen on the *War Knight* were also awarded medals. Chief Engineer David Falconer and Apprentice Reginald Curtis Clayton received posthumous Albert Medals after succumbing to their burns in hospital.

On March 29, 1919, Chief Engineer Falconer was recognized for his gallantry.[43] Despite being badly burned, he prevented fire in the engine room by closing the skylights, rescued men succumbing to the fumes below deck, and gave up his own lifebelt to save a fellow crew member.

Apprentice Clayton, aged twenty, was recognized on August

---

[42] "Edward Stephen Fogarty Fegen VC," VC and GC Association, https://vcgca.org/our-people/profile/1651/Edward-Stephen-Fogarty-FEGEN.
[43] "Royal Navy & Merchant Navy Medals—Awards of the Albert Medal," Naval-History.net.

27, 1918,[44] for flooding the ammunition magazine of the *War Knight* immediately after the collision. He battled his way through the flames to reach the flood valve and was critically burned in doing so. His testimony was taken at his bedside in the hospital before he died of his burns. This brave young man stated after the fire had broken out that he "went to his fire station and flooded the magazine." He then added that he "only did his duty."[45] Without his prompt action, the magazine would have exploded and "it is probable that, as a result, the very few survivors who escaped would also have lost their lives."[46]

My faith in humanity remains firm when men of such valor live among us.

Fig. 22. The Gallantry/Albert Medal awarded posthumously to Apprentice Reginald Clayton[47]

---

[44] "Royal Navy & Merchant Navy Medals—Awards of the Albert Medal," Naval-History.net.
[45] *Court of Enquiry Order 0197/62, 532.*
[46] *Court of Enquiry Order 0197/62, 532.*
[47] "Deep Sea Diving: Wreck of the *War Knight*," September 5, 2022, https://divernet.com/scuba-diving/deep-sea-diving-in-the-wreck-of-ss-war-knight/.

INSURANCE CLAIMS

Where risk to life and large sums of money and property are involved, the insurance concept is used to spread the risk among as many people as possible so that any loss is lower for all. Owners of merchant ships during World War I were in particular need of such insurance. Without some assurance, ship owners were reluctant to expose their large investment in ships and the cargo they carried to the risk of not just marine peril but war peril as well.

Toward this end, the British government created the War Risks Insurance Office (WRIO) in 1914 to provide insurance to British ships and cargoes against the risks of both war and marine perils during World War I.[48] Their mission was to ensure that British shipping continued to operate during the war. This was essential to the British economy as shipping was the main way that goods were imported and exported. The WRIO played an important role in supporting the war effort by providing insurance to ships that were transporting troops and supplies. The WRIO proved to be a very successful innovation by the British government.

The owners of the *War Knight*, Furness, Withy & Co., were insured by the WRIO, and they were understandably concerned as to whether the collision of the *War Knight* and *O. B. Jennings* would be deemed by the UK Admiralty to be the result of a war

[48] Most available online sources reference the US Bureau of War Risk Insurance. Searches at Hansard.parliament.uk for "War Risks" from 1914–1918 renders a broad view of the debates in the UK Parliament, which informed the creation of the government insurance scheme and the clubs which filled the gap, in particular UK Parliament House of Commons, "War Risks (Insurance)," Volume 66: debated on Wednesday, August 26, 1914, https://hansard.parliament.uk/Commons/1914-08-26/debates/1899bbe2-8a45-44ef-bccc-3ae1bc6ec24c/WarRisks(Insurance) and "War Risks (State Insurance)," Volume 66: debated on Thursday, August 27, 1914, https://hansard.parliament.uk/Commons/1914-08-27/debates/910754e5-7c3f-4da8-9027-b41117ca31ab/WarRisks(StateInsurance).

risk, a marine risk, or both. In the final letter in the Admiralty file from the UK Admiralty to the WRIO, the decision rendered was that the collision was the result of marine risk only.

This decision raised a considerable amount of controversy within insurance circles and merchant-ship owners. Furness, Withy & Co. were ultimately compensated by the WRIO for only part of the loss of their ship. Despite the UK Admiralty's ruling of maritime risk only, the WRIO determined that *War Knight*'s position in the convoy, which was subject to potential enemy action, constituted a war risk. This decision was based on the fact that the convoy had been warned about possible German submarine activity in the area, and the course of the *War Knight* had been altered as a result.

The WRIO's decision was significant because it set a precedent for other war-related maritime losses. In subsequent cases, the WRIO was more likely to consider a loss to be due to a war risk if the vessel was part of a convoy or was otherwise susceptible to enemy action.

The total cost of the *War Knight*'s loss was estimated to be £250,000. The WRIO paid Furness, Withy & Co. £150,000, which was the maximum amount of compensation that the company was eligible for under its insurance policy. The remaining £100,000 was covered by the *War Knight*'s hull insurance.

The owners of the *O. B. Jennings*, Standard Oil of New Jersey, were more successful in recovering their losses. They initially sought compensation from the British government's WRIO on the grounds that the collision was a war risk, as the *War Knight* was part of an Allied convoy. However, the WRIO ruled that since the collision was deemed by the UK Admiralty to be a maritime risk only, they denied the claim.

Standard Oil then filed a lawsuit against Furness, Withy & Co., the owners of the *War Knight*, in the United States District Court for the Southern District of New York. The court found in favor of Standard Oil and awarded the company damages in the amount of $280,000.

Furness, Withy & Co. appealed the decision to the United States Court of Appeals for the Second Circuit. However, the court of appeals upheld the district court's ruling.

The owners of the *O. B. Jennings* were ultimately able to recover their losses through the court system. However, the process was lengthy and expensive. The case highlights the challenges that ship owners faced in recovering losses from collisions during World War I. The lawsuit was filed in 1918 and was not settled until 1923. The court found that the *War Knight* was solely responsible for the collision. The damages awarded to Standard Oil included the cost of repairing the *O. B. Jennings*, lost profits, and salvage costs.

World War I continued for the next eight months after the collision at its destined pace of stagnant trench warfare and convoys of ships bringing troops and supplies to feed this stalemated behemoth. But for the *War Knight*, the *O. B. Jennings*, my father, and all the others involved in the collision, the war stopped for ever-so-slight a moment for its players to absorb and try to make sense of this catastrophic event. As with all tragic moments during war, death and scars remained to be remembered with reverence and to be honored with sober and proper historical perspective.

CHAPTER 13

— ★ —

Final Disposition of the Ships

FATE OF THE *WAR KNIGHT*

The *War Knight* was stranded in Watcombe Bay near Freshwater on the Isle of Wight, where she was eventually "scuttled" to the bottom of the ocean and lies today at a depth of about thirteen meters.

Fig. 23. The stranding of the War Knight

The wreck of the *War Knight* has been extensively studied and is a popular site today for professional researchers of wartime wrecks and scuba divers. The process of stranding the *War Knight* was photographed, and an amazing live film of its stranding is available at the Imperial War Museum Library website.[49] It shows the ship stranded in the bay until it is nearly covered by the rising tide.

The people living on the Isle of Wight were impacted by the stranding and scuttling of the *War Knight*. In 1934, Fred Mew published a firsthand account of what he saw of the wreck in his book, *Back of the Wight*. Mew lived on the Isle of Wight and spent much of his time on the coast and was a member of the Life Saving Apparatus Company, so he witnessed many shipwrecks on the coast. At the time of the wreck of the *War Knight*, he went down to the bay from Freshwater to investigate. The cliffs overlooking the scene gave him a good position to see what was happening.

The cargo—including things such as bacon, lard, flour, oil, and rubber—was spilt into the sea and washed up on the shore, and for weeks the area was busy with people finding all the salvageable cargo to take home. He says that at the time, because of rationing, people did not have much food at home—especially meat—so the bacon was especially popular among those on the beach. Even months after the wreck, he remembered that cargo such as lard could be found buried in the sand.

The people of Freshwater considered this a gigantic stroke of luck and carried crates of the remains away to their homes. However, the local police and customs officials decided at some point that the salvaging was unlawful and arrested thirty-eight people who had to travel by train to nearby Newport for trial and were subsequently fined a total of £411. The local police letters book for 1915–1919 lists awards given to three policemen for their work in arresting the salvagers. Two of the policemen were given a two-pound award for their work, and the third was given a five-pound award for his zealousness in making arrests. This might explain the sardonic name given by the locals to the train that took those arrested to Newport for trial—the "Bacon and Lard Special."

---

[49] Video available at "The Stranding of SS *War-Knight*," IWM 573, Imperial War Museums, https://www.iwm.org.uk/collections/item/object/1060023115.

Forty-five years later, bales of raw rubber from the *War Knight*'s cargo still washed up in Freshwater Bay, and beachcombers collected four pounds per bale in salvage money.

The story of the *War Knight*'s crew is one of the many tragic stories that fills the history pages of World War I. My father was directly impacted by their story, and now that I know it, it encompasses me as well. I know my father would join me in always remembering and honoring the *War Knight* and its brave crew.

FATE OF THE *O. B. JENNINGS*

After the collision, the *O. B. Jennings* was towed into Sandown Bay on the southeastern coast of the Isle of Wight, where she continued to burn for ten days. People on the Isle of Wight were able to observe and photograph the ship as it burned.

Fig. 24. The O. B. Jennings *on fire in Sandown Bay, Isle of Wight. If you look carefully, you can just see the aft of the ship and the smoking funnel.*
(Photo by Flight Sub Lt. Richard Alexander Nicholson thanks to Paul Donnellan)[50]

---

[50] "*O. B. Jennings* – (1917–1918)," Auke Visser's International Esso Tankers Site, https://www.aukevisser.nl/inter/id384.htm.

After ten days, the *O. B. Jennings* was finally scuttled by friendly fire. The decision was later made that the ship was repairable, and consequently, she was refloated in April 1918 and taken to a shipyard on the Isle of Wight for repairs. The repairs to the *O. B. Jennings* were extensive and took several months to complete.

Fig. 25. The O. B. Jennings *after being refloated with temporary repairs*[51]

The repaired *O. B. Jennings* was put back in service, and on her next voyage from Plymouth to Newport News, she encountered a submarine in the middle Atlantic on 4 August 1918.[52] The submarine attempted a submerged torpedo shot, but the try was unsuccessful, and the submarine had to surface to bring her deck gun into play. The crew of the *O. B. Jennings* fought back bravely for twenty-two minutes with their smaller

---

[51] "*O. B. Jennings* – (1917–1918)," Auke Visser's International Esso Tankers Site.
[52] "Oil Ship Crash," *New York Times,* August 6, 1918.

gun, but a shell from the submarine hit the *O. B. Jennings*'s magazine and put her gun out of action. At that point, the crew abandoned ship and took to their lifeboats. The submarine then closed range and sank the *O. B. Jennings* one hundred miles off the Virginia coast.

After sinking the *O. B. Jennings*, the submarine turned its attention to the crew adrift in boats. After interrogating the crew, the submarine captain took the second officer of the *O. B. Jennings* prisoner, after which the submarine cleared the area. The master of the *O. B. Jennings* had donned civilian attire and thus escaped capture.

Two members of the crew lost their lives in the encounter. The remainder of the crew was picked up by patrol boats and delivered to Norfolk.

It was a sad ending for the *O. B. Jennings*, the ship that played such a significant part in my father's life during five critical months of his Navy service.

CHAPTER 14

★

My Father's Succeeding Naval Assignments

USS *LAKE HARNEY*

Following the collision and my father's return to the Brooklyn Navy Yard, New York, on May 7, 1918, he was next assigned as an armed guard on the USS *Lake Harney*, a smaller ship with an interesting history. It was under construction in 1918 as *War Vigil* by the American Shipbuilding Company of Lorain, Ohio. The prefix "War" in the name indicates it was originally intended for purchase by the British government under the Standard Build Ships program. However, before the completion of its construction and launch on May 18, 1918, it was bought by the United States Shipping Board and renamed *Lake Harney*. It was acquired by the US Navy on July 27, 1918, and commissioned as the USS *Lake Harney* on the same day in Montreal, Canada.

I am not certain of the exact date my father joined this ship, but he was on its maiden voyage from Montreal to St. Nazaire, France, arriving there on August 3, 1918. There the ship was assigned to the Naval Overseas Transportation Service (NOTS) as a coal transport based at Cardiff, Wales. The ship operated between ports in England, Ireland, Wales, and France up to the armistice on November 11, 1918, and continued afterward until August of 1919.

MAIL FROM HOME—SOMEWHERE OVER THERE

While assigned to the USS *Lake Harney*, my father wrote a letter to his sister, my Aunt Gina. This letter is one of only two pieces of correspondence that remain to document my father's World War I Navy experiences. I combed this letter very carefully for hints and any new revelations of his character and personality. I was not disappointed by what I found. The letter revealed things about my father that I was not aware.

The letter was written on December 2, 1918, just a few weeks after the war ended. Despite the war having just ended, censorship must have still been in effect since he placed at the top of the letter "somewhere over there" as his location.

The letter was in classic form for any GI writing to the folks back home—sending news from him and seeking news from home. It was clearly meant for his entire family, but my father addressed the letter to his younger sister, Gina, knowing it would be widely shared. He had apparently received a batch of letters that day, one of which was from Gina, and he was answering it right away.

The following is a transcription of his letter with some editing to provide clarity and context:

Somewhere over there
Dec. 2, 1918

Dear Sister,

I received your letter today and I'm more than glad to hear from you now that the war is over. I will be able to tell you more than before.

I'm very sorry to hear of those deaths in the states, but [the Spanish flu] is something awful. I feel bad for other [not readable], but we can't help it. It's just as bad over here. I had a light attack of it myself, but I soon got over it.

And I also heard of Tony DiCarlo being killed in action. We get an American newspaper once in a while, and I always look for the casualties. That's where I found out of Tony DiCarlo being killed.

I was also glad to receive those pictures you sent me before I left N.Y. How I got them I will tell you. I wrote to the Fleet Post Office and told them to send my mail over here (Cardiff), and they were very kind to send it to me.

I am sending you a little Irish souvenir as I promised. I was in Belfast, Ireland, for about a week, and I didn't want to send them from there because I was afraid you wouldn't receive them. I am sending you two of them, and I wish you would give one of them to the boss of the cardroom [in the Natick cotton mill] and [tell] him it's a souvenir from Ireland. I would like to write to him, but I don't know his full name and address.

I wrote to Cousin Annie last night—the one that got married lately.

I would like to tell you where I've been but that will take too long to write, and I have lots of letters to write tonight. I received quite a few letters yesterday and today. So, you see, I am feeling quite happy. But I will wait until I get back home although I don't expect to get back for a long time. And please tell Mother not to worry as we are both all right. I will close hoping this letter will find you all in good health. Give my love to all the folks.

From your dear brother,
GM2c Michael A. Tedeschi
USS *Lake Harney*
c/o Port Commander, Cardiff, England

Allow me to expand on the letter and interpret between the sentences. I picture my father on the USS *Lake Harney* located in some unknown port in Europe with a batch of mail that just recently caught up with him through the Fleet Postal Service. He picked out the letter from his sister, Gina, to answer first.

He starts out by regretting that he could not relate more of his wartime experiences in past correspondence because of censorship rules. He is obviously anxious to share these experiences now that the war is over because he has so much to tell. I can only imagine the store of World War I experiences my father wants to share.

He next writes about the Spanish flu pandemic then sweeping the world. Gina must have written in her letter about the large number of deaths occurring at home, and my father laments this and expresses resignation in the failure to stop its spread all over the world.

His next comment is about discovering that a hometown acquaintance, Tony DiCarlo, obviously known to Gina and the other members of his family, was killed in action. (I recall a small stone monument that was placed in a street-side plaza not far from our home in Rhode Island. Its bronze plaque listed the names of the three men from Natick that were killed in World War I. One of the names was Anthony "Tony" DiCarlo.) My father remarks on the serendipity of discovering this information when his only chance of gaining such knowledge was by scrutinizing casualty lists published in American newspapers—which he was only occasionally able to obtain and read.

Expressing delight when he received photos in this letter, my father felt it was necessary to explain to his sister why the letter was delayed in reaching him. My father had been receiving mail again at the Brooklyn Navy Yard following the collision and his return to the US for reassignment to the USS *Lake Harney*. His mail, received after the USS *Lake Harney* sailed, was collected and forwarded to him by the Fleet Post Office to his new base in Cardiff, Wales.

He next writes about sending Gina two Irish souvenirs he bought in Dublin—one for her as he had previously promised her, and one for "the boss in the cardroom." He is referring to a person who works in the Natick cotton mill who was known both to him and Gina. He is asking Gina to deliver this gift for him since she is still working at the mill and because my father did not remember the man's full name and address.

This request reveals to me an insight into my father's character and his caring nature. I am impressed and at the same time curious that he would remember the Irish boss in the mill's cardroom some two years and eight months after he departed his job there to join the Navy. Why would my father make such a gesture of kind regard to acknowledge and respect someone's Irish roots and background—especially a relative stranger? I suspect there is more to the story, because it does not accord with the subtle ethnic tensions that existed between the Irish and Italian workers at the mill.

The cardroom was the part of the mill where, in the first stages of cotton manufacture, the raw cotton was "carded" by a machine with rollers covered with metal spikes used to brush, clean, and disentangle the short fibers of cotton in preparation for spinning into thread. The supervisors and managers in the mill were mostly of English or Irish descent, and this was the case in the cardroom at the time my father began his work at the mill as a youngster of eight or nine years old. He later moved up to work at a spinning machine that turned the cotton coming out of the cardroom into thread.

While growing up, I remember the grown-ups' discussions of the small tensions that existed between the various ethnic groups making up the workforce at the mill. I have memory of a story told that young boys, mostly of Italian descent who worked in the cardroom, did all the grunt work. They were the ones who removed the cotton from the shipping bales and fed it into the carding machine all under the supervision of older men mostly of Irish descent. Most of the boys did not wear shoes, and it was the big joke of the tobacco-chewing Irish to spit at the bare feet of the boys working there!

There may be only shreds of truth to this apocryphal story, but it is against this background that I ponder why my father made this extraordinary gesture of sending a souvenir gift from Ireland to his former Irish boss in the cardroom. I want to believe that my father rose above any ethnic animosities and made a gesture of amends and goodwill in doing so.

His next reference in the letter is a commonplace acknowledgment that he wrote a letter (of congratulations?) to a first cousin named Annie who was recently married. This tells me my father was family oriented and respected important family events.

In his concluding paragraph, he expresses a lament that he would like to write more and tell Gina of all the places he's visited, but that it would take too long to do so, and he is pressed by all the other letters he has just received and wants to answer them. He then exclaims that he is feeling "quite happy" about all the mail he has just received.

I am thrilled even today as I write this to know of this point in time in my father's life when he declared he was "quite happy." How I wish I could have talked about it with him sometime, especially after my Vietnam experience, when I, too, knew the joy of receiving overseas mail from home and how much it meant.

In his final thoughts in the letter, my father expresses the reality that it will be a "long time" before he returns home. I am certain that my father was aware that there was a great push to bring the troops home after the war was over. However, he also recognized that the Navy still needed the resources to man the troop ships bringing them home. It would be eleven more months before he returned.

He then adds the consoling thought for his mother "not to worry as we are both all right." Here he recognizes that his mother had two sons serving in the military and that both he and his older brother Jimmy (in the Army) have survived the war and will be returning home unharmed.

This letter is very precious to me. I can feel the emotion and thoughts that went into the letter, and it has helped me to bond with and know my father better.

After the armistice, the foreign contingent of ships in the Naval Overseas Transportation Service began to be withdrawn from duties. USS *Lake Harney* returned to the US and was decommissioned on August 26, 1919, and given back to the United States Shipping Board. My father stayed aboard the USS *Lake Harney* for the full twelve months of its active service with NOTS.

USS *PHILIPPINE*

My father's service record next indicates that following his release from the USS *Lake Harney*, he was temporarily held at the Brooklyn Navy Yard Receiving Station until assignment to the USS *Philippine*. This was an older ship that had already accumulated a long and interesting history of service.

Originally named the SS *Bulgaria*, she was a passenger-cargo steamship built in 1898 for the Hamburg America Line. In 1899, after only a few months in service, she was caught in a severe hurricane and disabled mid-ocean for some weeks. Her captain and officers were later decorated for their conduct saving lives and the ship during a truly harrowing battle between man and sea.

After this, the *Bulgaria* settled into regular service between Hamburg, Germany, and various ports in the US until 1913, when she was bought by Unione Austriaca and renamed SS *Canada*. After making only two trips between Trieste [then part of Austria, later Italy, and finally Yugoslavia] and Canada with this company, the ship returned to service with the Hamburg America Line, reverted to her original name, and made a number of trips on the Hamburg–Boston–Baltimore run.

The *Bulgaria* completed her last voyage to Baltimore on July 27, 1914, a day before the outbreak of World War I. She laid up in Baltimore for almost three years until the entry of the US into the war in 1917. She was seized by the US, renamed the USAT (US Army Transport) *Hercules* (later renamed the USAT *Philippine*), and used as an animal and general cargo transport by the Army until the November 1918 armistice.

Recognizing the need to quickly return US troops from Europe, the Navy began to rapidly expand its troop transport fleet in the postwar period. To meet this need, a total of fifty-six ships, including the *Philippine*, were selected for conversion into Navy troop transports. The conversion took place in Hoboken, New Jersey, and on May 1, 1919, while still undergoing conversion, she was transferred to the US Navy and commissioned as the USS *Philippine*.

The ship had a crew complement of twenty-five officers and 168 enlisted men, as well as a troop-carrying capacity of eighty-six officers and 3,940 enlisted men. With my father as a member of the crew (no longer an armed guard), the USS *Philippine* made two round trips to France to repatriate US troops. In total, the ship returned 4,142 soldiers to the US on these two voyages.

POSTCARD FROM PARIS

My father wrote his second piece of surviving correspondence documenting his World War I Navy experiences while aboard the USS *Philippine*. It was a postcard from Paris, which he sent to the same sister, Gina. The postcard is not dated, but it is written while the USS *Philippine* was on its second and last voyage to France to repatriate troops. The short message on the postcard reads:

> Dear Sister,
>   I am sending you this card because it looks so much like you, and I thought you might like it. Every ship that's making the last trip to France gets a leave to Paris. So that's why I'm getting mine.
>
>   M.A. Tedeschi

Fig. 26. Image on reverse of postcard resembling my Aunt Gina

What a beautiful sentiment to send to his sister! It reveals a nature of my father he never openly showed to me. The picture on the reverse of the postcard is a girl of classic beauty, and even today, I can see some of his sister, my Aunt Gina, in it.

In his last sentence, he seems to want to explain why he is so fortunate and excited to be writing a postcard from Paris. I have been to Paris numerous times in my life, and I would want to share his excitement. I wonder if my father and I visited the same landmarks and tourist sites.

This was his last voyage. What was it like ferrying US troops home after the war? He must have had even more interesting experiences, more tales to relate. As a former professional soldier and military man, I would love to have heard the details firsthand from him. He never spoke to me about his wartime experiences, and I rarely heard him talk to others about them either. I know he had so much more to tell me. I really regret this omission in my life and feel disappointed even today that I was denied this opportunity by his early death from cancer at age fifty-seven.

Upon returning from the second trip from France to the US on September 26, 1919, the USS *Philippine* was decommissioned in October and transferred back to the US Shipping Board. The timing of these events coincides with the date of my father's discharge from the US Navy shortly thereafter on October 20, 1919, at Newport, Rhode Island. With the war over, the troops had returned home from France, my father had completed his military service, and he was ready to resume civilian life.

CHAPTER 15

★

After the War

My father never returned to the Natick cotton mill for work. He had learned new skills in the Navy, and he sought to use them when he returned home. Prior to marrying my mother in 1925, he became a truck driver, which led to his work for a wholesale beer distributor. In 1941, at the outbreak of World War II, he obtained US civil-service employment at Quonset Point Naval Air Station maintaining aircraft armament. He held this position until his death in 1951 from esophageal cancer.

Some of the aircraft armaments on which he worked started their scheduled maintenance with a dip in a bath filled with solvent. It's surmised that my father, after ten years at the job, had breathed in significant amounts of the vapors from the solvent, which led to his cancer. Health and safety codes that might have prevented his illness were implemented later.

My father had surgery to remove the cancer in 1950. He convalesced for a year and even returned to work at Quonset. During this time period, I naively failed to recognize the seriousness of my father's illness. The excitement of high school years blocked my understanding of cancer and death.

I describe the events and timing of my father's death in my companion book, *A Rock in the Clouds: A Life Revisited*. The two-year period, 1951–52, encompassed my last two years of high school at the same time my father was diagnosed and eventually died from cancer. Following is an excerpt from that book:

> The month of September 1951 was a hectic time for me. I started my senior year in high school, practiced football, and seemed to make almost daily visits to my father at the Veteran's Hospital in Providence. I don't know if I can do justice to the week and day my father died at the end of September. We had stayed at the hospital until very late the night before and left to get some sleep, then returned the next morning. I still thought my father would recover. They let me see him only once, but he was in a coma, and I guess I've tried to erase this memory all my life.
>
> When we arrived early the next morning, I rushed to his room while my mother and siblings, Mike and Theresa, delayed in the waiting room. When I got to his room, it was empty. I asked a nurse where they had moved my father. She did not give me an answer right away, but after some time, she told me my father had died.
>
> I dashed back to the waiting room and told my mother, brother, and sister. What a terrible moment. A doctor came by and told us the details. We left the hospital in pain and agony.
>
> The wake and funeral should have been overwhelming for me, but somehow, I held up better than most of my family. I was still naive, immature, and basically could not take in what was happening. I really didn't know how to act at that time.
>
> I missed one season football game (we easily won 52–0) and was back in school right away. It was probably the best thing for me. I remember crying, but the full impact of my father dying was still beyond me. I thought the more I occupied myself, the sooner the impact would

go away. Today, I know how badly I was in need of some help and counseling. But things were different then. You didn't fold—you were stoic and "manly." We just didn't have the luxury of counseling then.

For the remainder of that fall, I focused on school and football. As the captain of the football team, I was fully caught up in the excitement of a very successful season. We ended the season in a three-way tie for the RI State Class C Football Championship. I was sorely disappointed not to have my father at each of the games as the season progressed, and the painful memory is still with me.

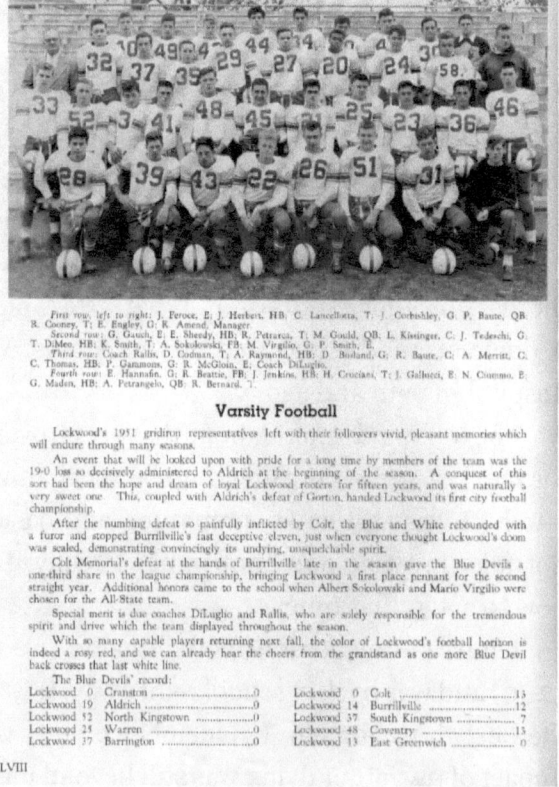

Fig. 27. Lockwood High School yearbook entry for 1951 season photo and recap

The last game of the season was played at East Greenwich, which we had to win to claim our share of the three-way tie. We did win, but it was a very tough game.

I cried on the bus going back to Lockwood. Somehow I knew this was the end of something big and final for me, and my father was not there to share it with me. It was a turning point in my life.

The harsh reality of my father's death finally hit me as I approached graduation from high school and looked to the future. I realized that without my father, my family was not in a position to finance a college education for me. This led, with the determined help of my sister, Theresa, and my football coach, Dom Diluglio, to a two-year long application process seeking an appointment to West Point. I eventually won the appointment and entered West Point in 1953.

I know my father would have been very pleased and proud of his youngest son's appointment and eventual graduation from West Point in 1957. I still wish I could have shared these moments with him.

CHAPTER 16

Knowing My Father

Researching my father's early life has been truly cathartic. I really feel that I got to know him better, especially by reliving his World War I experiences. I greatly admire his courage for the major life transition he made from running a spinning machine in a small-town cotton mill to enlisting as a sailor in the US Navy during wartime. His fourth grade education did not limit his ambition nor his striving for adventure and something better in his life.

As a first-generation son of immigrants, I believe he saw the opportunities being offered by the American Dream and qualified himself to pursue these opportunities by enlisting in the Navy at the outbreak of World War I. He certainly must have been a changed person when he returned from his service in the Navy to his small town of Natick.

In retrospect, I would have liked to have been there to welcome him home and to thank him for his service. I would also want to have thanked him for the opportunities he opened for me, his second-generation youngest son, and expressed to him the love and admiration we shared for our great nation.

The pain at the loss of my father when I needed him most became obvious as I recorded this search to know him better. My pain has been reconciled over the years, and I have found comfort and closure of this dark chapter of my life through my Catholic faith. I look forward to reliving that exciting high school football season of 1951 all over again with my father! I also want to know exactly how he escaped the burning *O. B. Jennings* and what it was like to be in the ocean surrounded by ignited gasoline.

In the meantime, I offer a much belated "Well done, *Poppa*, well done."

Fig. 28 Undated photo of my father taken some time in the 1940s

TRIBUTE TO THOSE WHO GO DOWN TO THE SEA

A war is never ended until the last story is told. This story is about a wartime event that took place 105 years ago during World War I, but it became alive and fresh for me when I was able to place my father in the narrative and describe the collision of the *O. B. Jennings* and *War Knight* as he might have experienced it. I hope my father will forgive me for any arrogance, but I feel I know more about the collision of the *O. B. Jennings* and *War Knight* than he ever did!

My search to know my father better through this retrospect of his early life and military service was very successful and rewarding, and I thank you, dear readers, for allowing me to share it with you. Researching and writing this book allowed me to better know and understand my long-lost father and to pay tribute to all the brave men who risk their lives going down to the sea in ships during time of war.

Fig. 29. My father's military grave marker

ACKNOWLEDGMENTS

This book began as a search to know my father better, but it quickly evolved. More than recording a tragic World War I naval accident that involved my father, the information I located revealed informative and intriguing aspects of naval history that are at the same time memorable and sad.

Once again, I had to "disappear" to my upstairs study to research and write this book, leaving my wife, Sue, and my other family members during that time. I thank them for their patience and forbearing, and in my ninety-first year, I want to assure them this book is my "last hurrah."

I could not have completed this book without the help and dedicated assistance of my longtime editor and guide, Shauna Queen Perez, who has taken me through two such book-writing ventures. Thank you, Shauna.

Thanks again to Koehler Books and their staff for accepting my manuscript and giving me another opportunity through their platform to tell this story.

www.ingramcontent.com/pod-product-compliance
Lightning Source LLC
LaVergne TN
LVHW041612070526
838199LV00052B/3109